Everyone Should Have
A Gay Son

Everyone Should Have
A Gay Son

A PASTOR'S JOURNEY

Rev. Dr. Jeri E. Williams

With Rose DeLone | Edited by Rev. Patricia Pitzer

Copyright © 2021 Rev. Dr. Jeri E. Williams.

All rights reserved. No part of this book may be used or reproduced by any means, graphic, electronic, or mechanical, including photocopying, recording, taping or by any information storage retrieval system without the written permission of the author except in the case of brief quotations embodied in critical articles and reviews.

This book is a work of non-fiction. Unless otherwise noted, the author and the publisher make no explicit guarantees as to the accuracy of the information contained in this book and in some cases, names of people and places have been altered to protect their privacy.

Archway Publishing books may be ordered through booksellers or by contacting:

Archway Publishing
1663 Liberty Drive
Bloomington, IN 47403
www.archwaypublishing.com
844-669-3957

Because of the dynamic nature of the Internet, any web addresses or links contained in this book may have changed since publication and may no longer be valid. The views expressed in this work are solely those of the author and do not necessarily reflect the views of the publisher, and the publisher hereby disclaims any responsibility for them.

Any people depicted in stock imagery provided by Getty Images are models, and such images are being used for illustrative purposes only. Certain stock imagery © Getty Images.

THE HOLY BIBLE, NEW INTERNATIONAL VERSION®, NIV® Copyright © 1973, 1978, 1984, 2011 by Biblica, Inc.® Used by permission. All rights reserved worldwide.

ISBN: 978-1-6657-0195-2 (sc)
ISBN: 978-1-6657-0194-5 (hc)
ISBN: 978-1-6657-0196-9 (e)

Library of Congress Control Number: 2021901363

Print information available on the last page.

Archway Publishing rev. date: 05/21/2021

Dedication

To Almighty God, my Prince of Peace, my Wonderful Counselor, and my best friend, Jesus the Christ

and

To my late husband, Larry, whom I love and can't wait to see in Heaven.

Acknowledgements

This book was a long time coming and very much a collaborative effort. The idea was birthed in 2008. It took me a while to gather my jumbled thoughts on the story. For two years, my dear friend and talented writer, Rose DeLone, sat with me every Friday night to listen to my experiences and put them in writing.

I am so grateful for her talent and skill in concisely expressing this story. My son John would go over everything with me on the phone. He would add, critique, develop, and email his input. I know God wanted me to put this in writing, even if just for one person to be moved from judgment to love.

I am so fortunate to have the encouragement of my Green Church family, who loved and fully supported me in this endeavor. Bob Pisel would edit grammar, Johanna Mickel would edit and endlessly type and retype additions and corrections, and Rev. Edward Harding, Jr., would do anything and everything to help in the process, without glory, to serve God.

I am thankful to those willing to share their stories, and for Steve and Jose who generously shared their work. I am so blessed to have three wonderful sons (James, John, and Andrew), my son-in-law Rody, Noreen, and Kay, who have loved and supported me all along. They are in the battle with me, and I am forever grateful.

I thank God for my precious brother Gary, my sister-in-law Allison, and my niece Nancy who bring great joy to my life every day.

I am also grateful to God for Angie, Shelley, Terri, Anthony, Ben, Mary, John, Pat, Carolyn, Karen, Sab, Dianne, Ed, Bob, Roe, Pat, Fred, Michele, Matthew, Annie, Jenny, Kathleen, Tony, Barb, Mike, Cathy, Dee, Sammy, Shawn, Tye, Linda, and Joan for providing places of escape and refuge when the pressure was overwhelming.

I am also grateful for my prayer partners Peg, Johanna, Julie, Karen, and Dianne, and to David, Daylan, Mark, Hannah, Rachel, Riley, Elizabeth, Michael, Jonny, Brianna, and Nathan.

Thank you:

- to Michele and Carrie for making me laugh,
- to Ed for teaching me perseverance,
- to Nicky for always helping,
- to my cousin Karen, because I know you are there just as Nancy would be,
- to Karen and John for your unwavering support, and
- to Mike, Colleen, Andy, Jake, Austin, Jeremy, Elizabeth, Pam, Jeannie, Linda, Lynn, Dan, John, Dan, Dennis, Joe, Linda, Joan, and Peggy for your wisdom and guidance.

Table of Contents

Introduction xi

Section 1: The Journey

1. I Had to Tell This Story 1
2. Nancy 4
3. Forever Changed 11
4. A Break from Tradition 14
5. The Battle Begins 20
6. From There to Here 25
7. Family Inspiration 29
8. "Jeri, I'm Gay" 33
9. The Decision 39
10. Stop the Hurt 42
11. Fusion or Confusion 46
12. Whose Agenda is This 53
13. A Seminary for All 55
14. Misplaced Intentions 58
15. An Amazing Child of God 61
16. Go Sleep with the Boys 64
17. The Boy in the Closet 67
18. A Price to Pay 69
19. Vision for The Green Church 76
20. Still More to Go 81
21. Why Should I Have a Gay Son 83
22. Apologies to the LGBTQ+ Community 85

Section 2: Stories of Transformation

1. Rose's Story 101
2. Johanna's Story 104
3. Steve's Story 107
4. Bob's Story 111
5. David's Story 114
6. Dan's Story 118
7. John's Story 121
8. Terri's Story 124
9. Jonathan's Story 128
10. Latifah's Story 130

Introduction

I urge everyone struggling with this issue to study the Bible and see what it says about homosexuality and gender.
- Rev. Dr. Jeri Williams

"How do you handle having a gay son?" It is the question everyone asks me. Whether I am at church, a conference, or even a party, it always comes up. No matter where I go, this question always finds its way into every conversation. Some people are genuinely curious, some are concerned for my spiritual well-being, and others are even sad for what they see as the loss of my son. Very rarely is anyone excited.

Since I am an American Baptist pastor, people assume that having a gay son must be devastating and contradictory to my beliefs. On some extremes, people even recommend conversion therapy or disowning my own son. It takes everything in me not to scream. I must constantly remind myself that we do not have the same experiences or the same backgrounds. They have not taken the same journey as I have – a journey that began long before I understood (or even gave a thought to) the issue of equality as it pertained to the LGBTQ+ community.

So when somebody asks me how I handle having a gay son, I take a breath, smile, and I always give the same answer: "I wish everybody was as blessed as I am. *Everyone should have a gay son.*"

SECTION I
THE JOURNEY

—1—
I Had to Tell This Story

It has been more than thirty years since my twins, John and James, were born. Thirty plus years of joy. Thirty plus years of laughter. Thirty plus years of pain. Thirty plus years of hope. But also, thirty plus years of fighting for John. Sometimes it seems like this fight is almost over, but as with every fight for equal rights, we take three steps forward and two steps back.

John is gay. I want him to live in a world where being gay does not define him as a human being. I want people to see him as I do, a funny, talented, caring person. Most importantly, especially as a mother, I want him to live in a world where he never has to fear for his safety, a world that accepts him for who he is through and through.

For many years, I pondered writing this book to tell this story. Every time I determined to move forward with the book, something groundbreaking would happen in society, and I would feel that this story did not matter, that the fight was over. When gay marriage became legal in 2015, I felt the battle had been won and the war was over. It seemed all the hurdles to equality had been cleared with this final milestone, and I could stop worrying for my son and the LGBTQ+ community.

Then in 2016, the presidential election became highly polarizing, bringing out the extremes in both liberal and conservative camps. Unfortunately, the divisiveness of the campaigns incited much anger and hatred toward the LGBTQ+ community. The day after the election, I was scrolling through my social media feed trying to make sense of what had happened, and came across my son's post:

> Rody and I don't often hold hands in public, and it's not because we don't like public displays of affection. It's because we grew up in a country where two men holding hands could be threatened, mocked, beat up, or even killed in a hate crime.
>
> Yesterday we learned that America does not side with us. America voted against the rights we have fought for and are still fighting to receive. The rights that are supposed to protect us.
>
> Muslims, Blacks, Asians, Native Americans, Latinos, the LGBTQ+ community, and women all feel different types of fear in America right now. We are afraid of being deported because of our religion, afraid of being raped, afraid of being killed by those who swear to protect us, afraid of having our land and water supply destroyed, afraid of losing our children and families.

One day I'd just like to hold the love of my life's hand in public and not be afraid.

Today is not that day.

My heart broke into pieces reading this, and I realized on a visceral level that the writing of this book was more important than ever. It was clear that, though we may have won a few battles, the war was far from over. Every story in this fight matters if it can help to change one mind or open one heart. I knew it was time to put it all down on paper.

I have laid out our family's story for the world to read in hopes that even just one person, one parent, can relate to what I have been through. I hope you can learn something from my journey.

2

Nancy

I cannot talk about my relationship with my son, or anyone else for that matter, without first talking about my relationship with my sister Nancy. From our early childhood through our teen years, Nancy was my best friend in the world. We had separate bedrooms, but Nancy always stayed in mine (or I in hers) so we could spend our nights talking and laughing. As one might imagine, the older we got, the longer those late-night chats became. We all know that teenage girls can talk about virtually nothing for ages! We would play our guitars and sing together for hours on end. Music was such an integral part of our personalities and our bond. Our favorite song was "Stairway to Heaven" by Led Zeppelin. We would record ourselves playing it (in its entirety) and laugh hysterically at the outcome.

Nancy and I were very different. I was a cheerleader going out with the captain of the football team, wrapped up in the popularity contest that so often defines high school. Basically, I was your typical high school cliché, with a focus on self-image and conformity. Nancy, on the other hand, had vastly different interests. While I cared about boys and cheer routines, Nancy was busy caring for and about other people. Not only was she in the band and the honors society, but she also found time to volunteer at a mental health facility helping patients cope with their daily struggles. She was an active member of the church, serving as the president of the youth group and a part of the choir. Nancy spent most of her time taking care of others, and I was one of those "others" who received much of her time and caring. She would listen to me for hours as I told her my latest dramas, triumphs, and heartbreaks, always ready to comfort and console me. Though now I can see how minor those issues were, she treated each and every one as if it was the worst or best thing that could ever happen to me. The topics were not important to her, but I was important to her – and she made sure I knew that.

One Saturday night when I was fifteen years old, I went to a party at a friend's house. When I got home around midnight, Nancy had just gotten in from a date. As usual, we sequestered ourselves in her room and spent the night together talking until about two in the morning about every detail of the party I attended and the date she had. This was not good planning for the daughters of a church pastor, as we knew full well that we would have to be up bright and early for church the next day.

In the morning as we dragged ourselves out of bed to get ready for church, Nancy said she had a headache and did not feel up to going. I was extremely irritated because I was just as tired from staying up late. It was not fair that she got to stay home and catch up on her sleep while I had to be on my best behavior, in my best clothes, for church. I thought she was such a good actress.

However, when we got home from church, Nancy was still in bed. I went in to see how she was feeling. She told me her friends had called to hang out with her, and she did not feel well enough to go out. That was not like Nancy. Hanging out with her friends was always a priority for her. But I did not give it much thought. I sat and talked with her for a little while longer, like I always did. A few hours later when we checked in on her, she was not able to move her head. My parents called the doctor. He told them to call an ambulance immediately. Suddenly my reality shifted. This was no act; this was very serious. I was worried – very worried.

I stood at the base of Nancy's bed while we waited for the ambulance. I thought I could talk her out of this, not wanting to let go of my notion that this was still an act. I kept shaking her foot and saying, "Nancy, come on. There's an ambulance on the way." I kept saying that over and over, but Nancy was not responding. The ambulance finally arrived and rushed Nancy to the hospital. Nancy had slipped into a coma, and I was overwhelmed with fear.

Nancy was in the ICU for the next week, and I visited several times a day – as much as I could while still trying to keep up with my studies. The ICU was packed every day with friends from school, the deacons of the church, and family members. Nancy always cared so much for other people and it showed. So many people were there to support her and to care for her now. I was astounded by the number of concerned people pouring through the door to her room at the hospital every day. They were praying for her and us, offering us unbelievable support and comfort. I cannot remember every face there, but I know for certain that without their constant kindness, my family would not have made it through this ordeal.

After about a week, we got the call from the hospital, which we had been praying for. Nancy had awakened. The rush of joy and relief my family and I felt was immeasurable. We got to the hospital as fast as possible. Nancy was awfully weak, but she was able to talk, which for me was a gift I had longed for that entire week. She told me that she was having a rough day. Confused by her comment, I asked why. "For starters," she explained, "the nurses cut my nails and took off my purple nail polish!" She loved that color. Nancy was never overly concerned about appearances, but she always had the gift of making others feel at ease by making light of the situation. We both chuckled at her sharp wit.

Then she became a bit more serious. She told me that when she woke up, she tried to rip all her tubes and needles out and get out of bed. As she tried to walk out of the room, all of the machines from which she thought she had untethered herself, were still attached to her. Unfortunately, they came along as she walked toward the door, tumbling on top of her and knocking her to the ground. She was so frustrated because she ended up chipping a tooth! I will never forget the look of horror on her face when she looked in the mirror and saw a big, chipped tooth front-and-center in her smile. Nail polish is one thing, but a chipped tooth, even in her mind, was unacceptable. She felt utterly miserable, but I was so immensely happy to have my best friend back.

Despite the fall and the chipped tooth, Nancy was doing exceptionally well that day. Even the doctor was excited by her improvement. Erring on the side of caution, he told us she would be moved to a regular room and out of the ICU, but not until the next day. It did not matter to me what room she occupied, I just rejoiced that her effervescent personality had returned, and she was just as funny and caring as ever. The feeling that I almost lost her was now behind me. I was ready to go back to our late night heart-to-hearts in our rooms, laughing and gossiping about boyfriends, classmates, fashion, and all other earth-shattering matters of teen culture. I said goodbye to Nancy so she could get some rest, and told her I would be back right after school that next day.

The following day school dragged on for what seemed like an eternity. When the bell finally rang, I raced home so I could go see my sister. Now that she was on the road to recovery, I wanted to make up for the time we had lost while she was in the coma. When I got home the house was empty. I was furious because I assumed they all left without me. Then I heard something in the basement. I went down the steps and peered around the corner to find my father sitting alone in his office crying.

I had never heard my father cry before, so I was instantly terrified. I hesitated, not knowing if I should make my presence known to him. Yet, I desperately needed to know what had thrown him into such grief. I slowly walked into the room, and cautiously asked him what was wrong. He told me that Nancy had slipped back into a coma.

My father was a very matter-of-fact person. After he regained his composure, he began preparing me for the worst. He told me there was a chance Nancy may never come out of the coma, or worse, she may die. My world was spinning out of control. How could she be lucid and even entertaining one day and facing death again the next? I could not listen to him. I insisted that Nancy would pull through. He spent his whole life preaching about HOPE and I was not going to let him give up on hope yet.

The next few days were spent at the hospital, visiting with and talking to Nancy. I told myself she had to pull through. I would not allow myself to believe she would slip away from us. I willed her to wake up just like she had before. I would make fun of her chipped tooth, hoping my cajoling would anger her enough to make her speak. I painted her nails purple again, expecting that simple act would make her smile and say thank you. But no matter what I tried, she remained silent and still. I could not understand why this was happening, and fear was mounting in my heart by the minute.

Amid the chaos of Nancy's health, life was moving forward whether we liked it or not. I returned to school physically, but not mentally. A few days had passed since Nancy slipped back into the coma. I was sitting in Algebra II class. I have never been able to pay attention in any math class, but on that day it was especially challenging. Thoughts raced through my mind as I was thinking about what Nancy and I would do once she got better. So much had happened in the days since she had fallen ill. I could not wait to talk to her about all the wonderful people who had come to the hospital to see her. I would fill her in on everything she missed, who kissed whom, who broke up with whom. I just knew she would recover because she was too young and too wonderful to die.

I started writing a note to my boyfriend to distract myself. As I was writing, there was a knock at the classroom door. A student came in and told the teacher that I was wanted at the principal's office. My friends turned and looked at me and we all smiled. I jumped out of my seat because I knew that Nancy must have come out of the coma. I knew for certain that I was getting my sister back!

As we walked down the hall, my smile broadened with each step as I anticipated the hours of conversation ahead with Nancy. We passed Nancy's locker, and I could not contain my excitement at being able to pass notes through the slots on the front again. What an incredible day. I was on top of the world.

As we entered the main office and passed the front desk, the secretary gave me the strangest look. We walked into the principal's office, where my mother and father sat waiting for me. The shades and blinds were all drawn; the principal walked out of his own office and closed the door behind him. Filled with hope, I looked at my parents expectantly and realized that they were not smiling. I froze.

My father looked me in the eyes, and with three words, changed my entire life.

"Nancy passed away."

3

Forever Changed

In the blink of an eye, I was lost. What was I going to do? There would be no more nights spent talking to my sister. We would never cringe about her chipped tooth; I would never get to tell her all that happened in the past week; I would never get to tell her anything ever again. Nancy was supposed to wake up. We were supposed to go home and paint her nails purple. But now that purple nail polish would sit on her dresser waiting, never to be opened again. I did not just lose my sister... I lost my best friend.

This had to be a dream; it just could not be true. But as reality sunk in, I began to scream at the top of my lungs. My parents just stood helplessly in the principal's office. They were as devastated as I was, but they were determined to be strong for all of us. With tears flowing uncontrollably down my face, my father walked me down the hall to get my belongings. Every step and turn of those corridors held a memory of Nancy. I could still see her leaning against that white brick wall by the music room waiting to walk in with her oboe, laughing with all her friends. As I approached my locker, I heard her laughter echo in the empty corridor; I sensed her rushing up just to say, "Hi," quickly as we both hurried to our next class. How could I ever traverse these halls again with these phantoms waiting everywhere to pull me into grief?

I continued to scream and cry as we came to my locker. I opened it, knowing there would be no more notes inside of it from my beautiful, thoughtful sister. I stood there for a while collecting my books and trying, unsuccessfully, to collect my thoughts. The whole school must have heard me by that point, as my cries echoed through the vacant halls. The entire experience was surreal, and I felt I could not distinguish between reality and illusion. We left the high school in slow motion. We picked up my younger brother, Gary, at the elementary school and went straight to the hospital.

As we entered the ICU, which just yesterday was filled with such grand hope, my body became numb. Every painful step I took towards her room felt like I had a thousand sandbags tied to my feet. I finally made it to her door and saw that there was no name on the front anymore. I walked into that cold, empty room. There were no more flowers, no more cards, no more machines, no more life. There was a white sheet covering Nancy's body, but her beautiful face was left uncovered. I walked up to her and touched her arm. It was icy cold, which shocked me more than I expected. My heart seemed to stop; my lungs failed to draw breath. I had to leave that room. I could not bear to see my best friend's lifeless body for one more instant.

Outside in the hallway, I waited. I could hear my parents crying over my sister, my brother standing with them not quite comprehending the situation at his young age. I could hear them sobbing for all of us, as if they knew I was too weak to even shed another tear and my brother was too young to understand grief.

My parents and my brother eventually emerged from the room. In silence, we made our way to the car and headed home.

As we rounded the corner to our house, I could see that the street in front of our house was brimming with people. All of Nancy's and my friends were outside waiting for us. The school had been closed early because so many students were devastated by Nancy's death. It seemed every single one of our friends had made their way to our house. My friends, Nancy's friends, and even people we barely knew, stood waiting to offer their condolences, hugs, prayers, and simple kindness to try to ease the pain we all bore deep in our souls.

My friends came running towards me when I got out of the car. We clung to each other and cried for what seemed like forever. For the first time in my life, I finally realized the importance of having a community of support and love. Let me repeat that, as it was a paramount turning point in my life: I FINALLY realized how important the love and support of community was! In that moment, it became crystal clear why Nancy liked going to church so much. Having a group of people who genuinely cared about what was happening in her life was critical to her physical, mental, and spiritual wellbeing. It bolstered her confidence, it heightened her compassion, and it certainly lifted her morale when she was feeling any kind of defeat.

I sat in my room that night, unsure of how I was supposed to act or feel, half expecting Nancy to walk in and plop down on my bed, as she always had. She never did. Nancy was gone. But I would never let her be forgotten. Nancy's entire life was spent caring for others, putting her own ambitions behind those of everyone she encountered. She lived outwardly, looking for ways to help another instead of ways to help herself. I was determined to do the same thing. In a moment of shear clarity, I vowed to live my life the way I know Nancy would have lived hers. I resolved I would become Nancy's legacy to this world.

4

A Break from Tradition

Though I wanted the world to leave me alone with my grief, I knew I had to move forward with as normal a life as I could. So, I did not stop partying with my friends. I still went out as much as I did before. I did not stop dating boys or talking about which ones were the cutest. I was still a teenager, after all. This is not a story about becoming a superhero, it is a story about being human.

Even though I was not involved in many church activities beyond Sunday mornings, I truly did love going to church, and I found it to be even more comforting in my time of grief. However, there were many things that did not sit quite well with me. I believe many Christians experience these same types of doubts and questions. People toss about all sorts of rules and regulations on how to live a more "godly" life. Don't do this and don't do that – no drinking, no dancing, no fun. These rules have never been a huge issue for me because I found it easy to disagree with them without it really affecting my life or my faith too much. I had a normal life. I went to church. I knew at my core that I was a good person; I knew that my heart was in the right place; I knew that God loved me and I loved God.

Years passed after Nancy's death, and life went on. I managed to return to school, in spite of the multitude of memories there that reminded me of my loss. After graduating high school, I went on to college to earn a degree in psychology. Saturday nights were filled with parties, friends, and fun. However, I was diligent about making it to church every Sunday. Weekdays I went to class, of course, but I also began volunteering at a prison, where I worked with inmates to help improve their lives. This was especially inspired by Nancy, and I know she would have done the same, if given the chance.

I found out quickly how much pain and sadness many of the inmates carried in their hearts. As they shared their stories with me, I could feel my heart breaking with every word. Their struggles were unimaginable. It became enormously apparent that psychology was not going to bring them the deep and all-encompassing healing they needed. I tossed aside the textbook and began praying with them.

The inmates I counseled wanted to find happiness and love, just as we all do. They dreamed of a life with white picket fences, a beautiful spouse, three kids, and a dog. Yet, they knew that would never be in the cards for them because, so often, the underlying issue was related to a drug addiction. So, naturally, I began volunteering at a drug rehabilitation facility.

I counseled addicts as they struggled to overcome the issues at the heart of their addiction. We talked about their lives, what brought them to this point, and why they felt they needed drugs. I got close to many of them. They often asked me to pray with them. I could talk ad nauseam about brilliant futures and getting out of their current situations, but nothing comforted them as much as praying together.

Week after week, we prayed. I could see so many changes in them. Attitudes shifted and each person, with whom I consistently prayed, moved from negative and depressed toward positive and inspired. It is impossible to explain the real power prayer brings to comfort people and ease their fears, worries, and doubts. I had experienced this at church after Nancy's death, and now I was able, in a way, to pay it forward.

The more I worked with these amazing people, watching their lives transformed through prayer, I realized I was being pulled into ministry. Growing up as a pastor's child, I certainly knew the peaks and valleys of being in ministry. But I never imagined I would be drawn to this servant life. Nevertheless, I knew it was the best way to help the many hurting and heartbroken people in this world. Now, for the first time ever, those rules that I basically chose to ignore suddenly became a real hurdle in my life.

Rule number one, and the biggest hurdle I faced, was that women were not permitted to be in the pastoral ministry. Women were allowed to hold traditionally female roles in the church, such as Sunday school teachers to children, church secretaries, or organizers of benevolence for the poor. But a woman could never lead a congregation. I had heard this all my life, and up until that moment, I had accepted and believed it as truth. Now I began to question this, and many other unwritten rules I had lived with all my life.

How could God lead me to a dead end? I knew God was leading me, but I was so conflicted inside. I felt strongly that, as a minister of God, I could make such an impact for God's kingdom here on earth. But how could I battle against the Goliath of the church that insisted women were not biblically approved to lead. I spent many hours in meditation and prayer, finally deciding to enroll in a master's program at a seminary. My end goal was to work in Christian education or counseling, which did not seem to challenge the teachings of the church. Upon entering the program, I found that I was one of only three women in the entire school.

One requirement for the Master of Divinity program was to write and deliver a sermon. The curriculum was developed for pastors, even though some of us were training for other types of ministry. Many of my classmates thought it was strange that I was required to do this, since it was not applicable to the real world. To be honest, I thought it was odd as well. But I wanted that degree, so I stuck to the program.

I reluctantly began writing my sermon, knowing how painful and tedious a process it was going to be. I had no desire to preach – that was not my objective. I concluded that I would simply complete this task, get it over with, and move on to the next step along the path God had laid before me. As I wrote, something wholly unexpected happened. The sermon I was composing seemed to flow seamlessly out of me. The pages piled up quickly. It was too easy. I knew something had to be wrong. In no time at all, and certainly not the hours of agony I had imagined, my sermon was finished. I read it repeatedly. Imagine my surprise when I realized it was good – it was actually GOOD!

The class and this assignment required me to deliver my sermon at the church where I was an intern. I was absolutely terrified. I practiced my sermon for the entire school year, memorizing it from front to back. Yet, no matter how much I practiced and memorized, I feared that the rejection of my message simply because of my gender would crush me completely. How could God put me up to such a humiliating task? It was clear, from all that I had been taught in church, that God did not desire women to be pastors, so why would God bring me to a point like this?

On the morning I was to deliver the sermon, the church was packed with approximately 2,000 people seated in the pews. As I looked out from the front, I saw my family, of course, and many of my friends from college, which was somewhat unexpected. Their support was of little consequence in my mind. I just prayed that I would not embarrass them in this undertaking.

Normally, a student would wear their own ministerial robe. Since I did not believe in a million years that I would ever need or wear one, I had not purchased one, as they are typically quite expensive. Instead, one of the pastors of the church graciously loaned me a robe. Thankfully, the style of clerical robes for this particular church was not highly tailored, so the fit was adequate for this one-time use.

Finally, the time came for me to deliver this message. I stood up and grabbed my papers. My hands were shaking so violently I thought the papers would fly right out of them and onto the floor. I steadied myself and marched up onto the platform. It was all I could do not to trip and stumble as I made my way to the pulpit.

Then something unexpected happened. As I began to speak, I felt as if I was in another body. I could hear my typically timid voice echo throughout the sanctuary. It was as if God were right there with me, helping me speak. It was clear that the words were not, and never were, mine. They were God's words, and God was determined these words would be heard. I delivered the sermon without a single stutter or hesitation. I was stunned, relieved, and filled with humble gratitude that the God of the universe would do this for me. It took every ounce of composure I could muster to calmly return to my seat and continue in worship until the end of the service.

When the service finally ended, my friends swarmed me, offering words of congratulations and admiration. I remember how shocked they seemed because I had never been good at public speaking. In college they would count how many times I would twirl my hair when I had to talk in front of the class. The record was 322 times. Picture their astonishment when they witnessed no hair twirling at all.

As I walked out of the church with my family, someone passed me and said, "That was pretty good for a woman!" I thought to myself, "You're damn right it was!"

5

The Battle Begins

After I graduated with my Master of Divinity degree, I took on the position of Youth and Children's Minister at Drexel Hill Baptist Church, just outside of Philadelphia, Pennsylvania. I was ordained shortly after joining the staff, which allowed me to be able to preach and teach all people in the congregation.

Despite my ordination and title of "Reverend," I was continuing my service in a role that was more acceptable for women, as the Youth and Children's Minister. Even though my name was preceded by "REV" and I was, by that title, permitted to take on more pastoral duties, it was less unsettling to everyone for me to maintain traditional responsibilities. I was fine with this because it was still a big step for a woman to have an official ministerial title, let alone get paid for it.

Not long after I began the job, the senior pastor asked me to visit one of our members in the hospital. This was my first time visiting a member alone in an official capacity as a minister of our church. Needless to say, I was a bit nervous. However, I was honored by the confidence the senior pastor had in me. I was up for the task.

When I arrived at the hospital, I pulled into the garage and parked in a space designated for clergy, making sure my placard was visible in the window of the car. I walked to the back doors of the hospital, which were for authorized personnel use only, and assertively swiped my clergy badge to unlock the door. Within seconds of entering, I was slammed against the wall and restrained by a security officer. The officer started screaming at me to tell him where I had gotten the badge, because he was convinced it had been stolen. No matter how much I explained my legitimacy, he could not believe that a woman could be a clergy member. He assumed I had stolen the badge in order to break into the hospital.

Eventually, the security officer permitted me to call the senior pastor. He explained the situation to the security guard, verifying that I was a valid member of the clergy and there at the hospital on official church business. Reluctantly, the security guard let me through, though he was not happy about it and most definitely was not about to apologize. In his mind, it was an egregious mistake – women should not be using that entrance.

I began to wonder how I would convince the world to fully accept me as an ordained minister. Did I have to cut my hair? Would I have to start wearing suits, or at least a collar? Should I lower my voice? I noticed that there were very few women ministers at the time, and most of them had assumed traditionally masculine demeanors in order to fit in. This was so difficult for me because I was such a "girly-girl." I embraced being and looking feminine. If I had to deny that part of me, it would be as if I were denying my true identity. The whole idea weighed heavily on me as I experimented with various options to overcome the overwhelming amount of sexism I was experiencing.

Another incident took place shortly after that, which caused me to re-evaluate my role in ministry, both locally and globally. I spent months organizing a youth mission trip to Puerto Rico. I planned every single detail for the trip, which I viewed as a huge accomplishment. The local newspaper took notice; they decided to do an article about it.

I was thrilled that my hard work was going to be recognized. This would be a public relations boost to the church. The senior pastor and I met with the newspaper so they could interview us about the story. The senior pastor was incredibly supportive. He sat quietly by my side as I answered all of the reporter's questions. I talked about the entire planning process, and what we intended to accomplish in Puerto Rico. Our main objective was to help clean up an old school that was in a severe state of disrepair.

I was overjoyed when the article came out, and I picked up several copies to take to the church. I wanted every member to read it and know that their own church, our little Drexel Hill Baptist Church, was making a difference in the world. I eagerly tore open the newspaper and began reading the article. As my eyes followed the story, my heart sank. All my efforts of planning, organizing, and budgeting had been attributed to the senior pastor. The newspaper wrote the entire article as though it was HIS project, how HE had organized everything about this trip. I was nowhere to be found, except for one marginal mention as the woman who helped fundraise. I felt woefully defeated, all because I was FEMALE.

At this point I knew I had to do something. It did not make any sense to me that people were so offended by women in ministry that they could not even bring themselves to attribute the standard duties of a youth minister to a woman. I knew God needed me to take a stand against this injustice. I made up my mind that I would go back to seminary to get my doctorate.

I began my doctoral program with one very important dissertation topic in mind: women in ministry. I did not need to investigate my direction or look at options as I proceeded with my classwork. From the start, the battle I was to fight for God's kingdom here on earth was very clear to me. I wish I could say that everyone was excited for me, but that was certainly not the case. More were against the notion than for it. I felt like David facing Goliath, and I do not like conflict. I am not sure if any woman had ever received a doctorate at this particular seminary before. All I knew was that I was the only one in the program now. I may have seemed outnumbered, but I knew God was on my side, and that meant losing was not an option.

I still was not sure if I believed that women could truly become pastors, so I began exploring the scriptures. I augmented my work with deeper study of biblical Hebrew and Greek languages so I could evaluate the Bible in its original language and context. This enabled me to derive more informed conclusions about the authors' intentions, rather than drawing conclusions from what I had always been taught or the ways others interpreted and translated the text.

I immersed myself in these studies, and I began to uncover gaping holes in the translations used throughout the church. There were so many instances where arguments could be supported either way. I discovered that the Bible was not as black and white as I had been led to believe my entire life. The black and white areas that I did find left me searching for more answers. I realized the scriptures can be interpreted in a plethora of ways. The more I dug, the more I discerned the Bible did not condone or promote exclusion at all. It spoke to me about inclusion of all people from all walks of life. It was as if God was speaking directly to me, and my doubts about the validity of women in ministry began to fade away. I knew, without question, that I was meant to be a pastor, as were many women gifted by God to teach and preach. The battle was ON, and I was going to lead the charge.

One day while my friends and I were sitting in the seminary dining area, the topic of women in ministry came up. I looked at this group of friends and realized not a single one of them supported me in my plan to become a pastor. They kept using one specific phrase claiming to care about me. They kept repeating this phrase ad nauseam. I had heard the phrase throughout my childhood and my time in seminary, "love the sinner; hate the sin." I was not going to give my entire life to do something that was a sin. I knew this was not a sin; I knew this was God's direction for my life and the lives of many women God had called and was calling into ministry. I knew they were going to have to concede. To this day, I cringe whenever anyone uses that phrase. I have vowed to never use it, instead responding, "Love the sinner, which is each of us, as God does!"

My studies, research, writing, and editing turned out to be quite a struggle. The process was slow and tedious, but with the support of many good people, I was able to complete my dissertation and receive my Doctorate in Ministry. Soon after, I was offered a promotion to Associate Pastor at Drexel Hill Baptist Church, and my career as a full-fledged pastor finally began. I slung that stone and the giant fell. I thought my days of fighting for the "underdogs" were over. Little did I know what God had planned.

6

From There to Here

As I mentioned before, I was ordained as an American Baptist minister at Drexel Hill Baptist Church in 1986. The 22,000 square foot church had close to 500 members. It was rich in Baptist tradition and continued to grow. There were three choirs (bell choir, adult choir, and youth choir), children's ministries, a nursery school, church council, and a variety of boards, including Trustees, Deacons, Christian Education, and Mission and Outreach. Everything ran smoothly and perfectly, like the proverbial well-oiled machine.

We had pastors, a church secretary, regular office hours, janitors, staff meetings, board meetings every Monday night, worship on Sundays, youth groups on Sunday nights, various Bible studies, and fellowship groups throughout the week. Our worship began beautifully with the organ prelude and the procession of the choir. We even had paid soloists and musicians. The church was busy, the ministries were fruitful, and the congregation was faithful.

All seemed perfect at Drexel Hill Baptist Church. Worship began promptly at 11:00, not 11:01, and ended precisely at 12:00. A clock hung in the back of the sanctuary to be sure the pastors were aware of the time. If you ran a minute over, there would be several people tapping their watches to let you know. There would even be a disciplinary meeting called if you went too long. Rules were made and meant to be followed. There was no bending allowed.

One September Sunday back in the late 1980s, as I stood in the traditional line at the back of the sanctuary where all good ministers greeted worshipers after service, a woman came to me with a request. "Jeri, the ladies of the Sunday school class would like to meet with you for a few minutes today after you are finished greeting everyone." I happily agreed to chat with them. I finished the receiving line and went to the fellowship room where several of the women had gathered. One of the ladies remarked, "Jeri, we have a concern." I saw all their heads nod in agreement. I was expecting some sort of dire need in the congregation or community that required immediate attention. However, I was quite surprised when she continued, "It's about your shoes.

"We've noticed that you are wearing white shoes and it's after Labor Day. Perhaps you were not aware that they are inappropriate after Labor Day and do not match your black robe." I assured them I would attend to it, and I vowed they would not see white shoes again until next summer. I must confess that ever since then, whenever I hear the word "concern" it is a red-flag warning that flashes in my mind.

I am certain that about now you are asking, "Why are you telling this silly shoe story?" It is simply because I want you to get a feel for what our church ideologies were when I began my ministry. We have come such a very long way from those days of the "fashion police."

As the years marched on, and fewer young families and adults were joining in traditional church life, our congregation, like many others, began to decrease. In 2011, the church moved to a new location more fitting to the smaller congregation and budget. Since we were no longer in the township of Drexel Hill, the name was changed to The Green Church, to reflect our mission to be excellent stewards of God's creation.

Fast-forward a few years to Christmas Eve, 2016. I was performing a wedding for an interracial male gay couple. Our beautiful little church was aglow with candles and twinkling Christmas lights, with poinsettias filling the sanctuary for the Christmas Eve wedding and candlelight worship service to follow. It was exquisite. Our tiny sanctuary was packed with wedding guests and church congregants. We were growing again and would soon be out of room to fit everyone. We thank God for these "problematic blessings."

One of my associate ministers was helping to lead the worship experience. Picture a six-foot-something, Black, gay man with a halo of Christmas lights atop his head and, of course, they were illuminated. He was joyously attired in lime green pants, lime green sneakers, and a lime green bow tie. He sang "O Holy Night" like an angel toward the end of the service, which brought a standing ovation. What do I consider the most amazing thing about this event? Not one word of judgment came from anyone in that church. I was filled with such gratitude that our congregation had exceeded any expectations I could have imagined, having endured an extraordinary transformation from what we once were. No more white shoe critiques here.

After service, we reconvened at the parsonage for a Christmas Eve and wedding celebration, enjoying food, wine, and precious fellowship into the wee hours of Christmas morning. We are truly a family celebrating our joys together. On Christmas morning, we worshiped, all decked out in our finest Green Church sweatshirts and jeans. Then we headed off to downtown Philadelphia to feed the homeless. What a perfect way to celebrate the birth of our Lord.

In my early days of ministry, Christmas Eve service would have commenced promptly at 7:00 PM and concluded by 8:00 PM sharp, with everyone immediately departing to be with their own families for their own festivities. That is when everyone in the congregation looked alike, not necessarily eye color or body type, but middle-class, Euro-Americans from suburbia. Now, the halo of twinkle lights, the diversity, the gay marriage ... back then, I would have been strung up by my toenails for choosing to celebrate in this unorthodox manner with these crazy, God-serving people. Today, it is just another day in the life of our wonderful church.

If it sounds like the voyage was easy getting to this place of freedom, celebration of diversity, and lack of judgment, it was far from that. Let me share with you some highlights of the journey.

7

Family Inspiration

My grandparents, John Stevenson Hall (for whom I named my son John) and Victoria Maude Hall, were missionaries. They lived in Africa with the Nigerian people, taught them about Jesus, and translated the New Testament of the Bible into their native language, Tangale. My grandparents were extremely well respected and loved there. The Nigerian Church in Kaltungo, which they founded, tells the story of 600,000 people who became followers of Jesus because of the example of these extraordinary servants of Christ. My grandfather is reported to have once baptized 7,000 people in a single weekend. His books on the pre-Christian spirituality of the Nigerian people are still read by anthropologists. The example my grandparents set of unconditional love and compassion, coupled with their knowledge of the Bible, still inspires many, myself included.

As a young girl, I was mesmerized by stories my grandmother told of her experiences with the African people. She showed me pictures of the huge cannibal pots that she passed every day in the village. Before they came to know Christ, the tribe she worked with would cook their defeated enemies in these gigantic cauldrons, a practice that was a very common assertion of dominance and victory among the tribes in this area of Africa. She recounted the painful stories of how her own children suffered from malaria, one of them even dying of whooping cough on the mission field. She felt the agony of loneliness and separation when she had to say goodbye to her eight surviving children as they were sent back to the United States, knowing she would not see them again for another four years, but knowing, too, they would be safe from harm and disease. I listened intently as a child to chronicles of her routine in this unyielding sub-Saharan landscape, including frequent encounters with poisonous snakes in her own house and yard.

Her day-to-day tasks were anything but routine, often including medical work treating hundreds of men, women, and children who would crowd daily into the dispensary for medication. Many times she would be the only missionary available to administer such help. She never related these stories as laments; they were simply the chronicles of her life and the work God had chosen for her.

There is a memory of one beautiful, sunny afternoon of storytelling that particularly stands out in my mind. Grandma and I sat together on the beach, the waves crashing hard against the sand. I could feel the salt in my hair as the breeze blew in from the ocean. She was sitting in her green and white fold-up chair wearing her straw beach hat, the bow tied neatly under her chin. I was lying on my towel next to her, enjoying the warmth of the sun and her company.

She was recalling her frequent three-mile walks in the intense sun to visit families in their mud huts. Contemplating her difficult and dangerous life, I sat up and posed this question, and I will never forget her answer. "Grandma," I inquired, "in all your hardships and hard work in that far away, hot country, didn't you ever doubt or wonder if God was always with you?" I remember her words as if she had spoken them yesterday. She turned her head, raised her eyebrows, and replied, "Yes I did, but I always knew that God promised never to leave me nor forsake me." That one simple reminder repeated throughout scripture still resonates with me today, and like Grandma, I hold onto it with all my strength. As she would always advise, we cannot keep our focus on the circumstances that surround us, we must keep our eyes on Jesus.

My grandmother's words echoed in my mind as I heard about the thousands gathered for the dedication of a 2,000 member church in memory of my grandfather, The John Stevenson Hall Memorial Church, and a hospital in honor of my grandmother. This church was built by the very people who were, at one time, cannibals. I was in awe of the Christian roots my grandparents planted so many years ago that still continue to grow and flourish.

As I began writing this book, I experienced an episode of doubt similar to what my grandmother faced. It was during my daily time of meditation that it occurred to me that my grandparents, Christians from a much older generation, most likely viewed homosexuality as a sin. A sense of dread washed over me. Would I get to heaven only to discover that they were ashamed of their granddaughter, who not only was a woman pastor (I am sure that probably did not go over well in their day), but fought for gay rights and named a school of ministry specifically for the gay community after my grandfather? Fear and dread filled me to the point of tears. What if I got this all incredibly wrong?

I spent many sleepless nights praying and agonizing over this plight. After months of tossing and turning, I finally received my answer while attending a charismatic retreat in Wildwood, New Jersey. I was dining with my dear friend, who also participated in these retreats. As we were enjoying our meal, I explained my struggle to her. We agreed to continue praying through the weekend for an answer. When we returned to the charismatic conference that evening, there was a choir from Nigeria who sang "What a Friend We Have in Jesus" in Hausa. Realistically, what are the odds of a choir from Nigeria singing one of my grandmother's favorite hymns at a Catholic charismatic convention in Wildwood, New Jersey? Tears filled my eyes. I felt as if my grandparents were singing directly to me. I looked at my friend and said, "I just got my answer." Indeed, God was guiding me, and still is. God would never leave me nor forsake me.

In 2017, I was honored to travel to Nigeria with my son James and my cousin Karen for the one hundredth anniversary of the arrival of my grandfather and his missionary colleague. The irony of it all was that our entourage was missing one family member who should have been there. My son John is named after my grandfather and the church established by him in Kaltungo. Yet, he could not go because of his sexual orientation. The danger of this trip for a gay man would have been far too great.

It was the ECWA (Evangelical Church Winning All) Kaltungo District Church Council Centennial Jubilee Celebration, commemorating one hundred years of God's faithfulness, or one hundred years of the coming of the Gospel in Tangale Land, Kaltungo (1917 – 2017). It was an unbelievable experience. I actually stood next to those tremendous cauldrons, which they have kept as a reminder of just how far they have come, spiritually. I could write another book on my experiences in Nigeria. However, the most important take-away from my trip was that my grandparents, and their oldest daughters Agnes and Margaret as well, gave their lives in service for a most important life changing mission, the spreading of the Gospel of Jesus Christ.

8

"Jeri, I'm Gay"

One of my very first experiences with the Christian homosexual community was with a gay man who sang in our church praise band. He loved God and was unbelievably musically gifted. Everyone loved him. One night after praise band practice, he asked to meet with me. As we climbed the stairs to my office, I could tell he was very anxious and upset. After we sat down in the quiet safety of my office, I asked, "Honey, what is wrong?" He replied, "I have to tell you something." I said, "I'm right here." He hesitated then exclaimed, "Jeri, I'm gay." I realized then how petrified he was, fearful of how I would respond. I reassured him, "Sweetheart, it makes absolutely no difference. I love you. And, more importantly, God loves you." He shared with me that he anticipated that this admission would mark the end of his days in the praise band at the church. He was certain I would not permit a gay man to lead our congregation in praising God. Nothing could have been farther from the truth. I was honored that he trusted me enough to talk to me about his sexuality. This experience helped me realize that we, as a church, had to actively take major steps toward inclusion and healing.

First and foremost, I realized we needed to become a welcoming and affirming church which publicly took a stand to support the LGBTQ+ community and their rights in society. And the time was now. However, it would not be an easy task. Voting was one thing, but we really had to have everyone on board with this new direction. It would be a transformational process, and a long road to get to where we needed to be. How would we, as a church family, and I, as a minister of Jesus Christ, get to the point where we were not only welcoming the LGBTQ+ community, but embracing them for who they are? How would this align with our American Baptist identity as a church? I was taught that if you are a Christian, you absolutely do not want to do anything that God says is a sin, or support anyone else who is sinning, either.

At that time, the official American Baptist stance was that homosexuality was "incompatible with Christian teachings." So I prayed and I studied the Bible because I wanted to be absolutely certain I was not taking others down the wrong path. Additionally as the pastor of this church, I was representing the American Baptist beliefs and teachings, something I did not take lightly. I had to be certain that I was not leading an entire congregation away from God's teachings and God's heart.

There were several members of the LGBTQ+ community in our congregation, and God gave me such a passion for their plight that I could not deny it anymore. The church was not a traditionally accepting place for them. Many churches adopt the "Don't ask, don't tell" approach, letting people side-step the issue. However, I wanted our church to be a place where everyone could be their authentic selves. I wanted everyone to be genuinely loved for exactly who God made them to be. That would take a tremendous amount of study, prayer, and work to accomplish. I was ready to take on the task.

It truly pained me that as a Christian and a pastor, I might inadvertently be helping to perpetuate a barrier in the relationship between members of the LGBTQ+ community and God. It was hard to fathom that I could possibly be, in part, responsible for millions of people not having a relationship with God because of judgment, hatred, and overt unkindness to them by the Christian community. I do not want to be part of any organization or group that excludes an entire community from the Kingdom of God.

I began pointedly asking God in my prayer times where there was a safe place for the LGBTQ+ community to love and serve their God? God was transforming Drexel Hill Baptist Church, but it was not there just yet. Hateful comments here or there could totally hurt and confuse the people we were trying to reach. We needed to be of one mind in this quest to embrace the LGBTQ+ community with the love of God.

By the early 2000s, my husband Larry and I were the co-pastors of Drexel Hill Baptist Church, where I had begun my ministerial career over a decade before. We were a church with a few hundred members just outside of Philadelphia, in a very "urban" suburb. One day, in particular, is prominent in my memory; it was a very important day for us as a congregation. Almost every adult member of our church had gathered to vote on officially becoming a welcoming and affirming congregation. If we voted yes, we would be the first in the area and one of the first Baptist Churches in the country to adopt that title. Welcoming and affirming is not a phrase used much today, but back in the late 1990s it was a very important designation. It signified that we not only welcomed the LGBTQ+ community into our church, but also affirmed that we believe their sexual orientation was inherent in the way God created them. They were not sinners; they were born that way. This was a notion that was rarely accepted in the church community at that time, and even still today. It would be a monumental declaration.

So, here we were. Over a hundred of us packed into a meeting room in the church meant to hold roughly fifty. People were sitting on tables and leaning against any object they could find. More people turned out for this than I could ever remember seeing at a congregational meeting. I could feel it in my gut that this was going to be a historic day, but tensions were high as we gathered to cast our votes. We had to have a unanimous vote, not a simple majority, in order to be considered a truly welcoming and affirming church.

The discussion in the meeting was a blend of uplifting speeches mixed with questions as to how this would affect our future as a church. The feeling in the room seemed to lean toward a yes vote, but there were several who still had their doubts. That is when I noticed one of our older members, whom I will call Robert, standing up. After waiting a few moments for the room to recognize him, Robert declared that he had something to say. Since he was from an older generation, this put me on edge. The older generation in our church often leaned much more towards the conservative side of the spectrum, and Robert was no exception. (Coincidentally, and to further illustrate the incredible journey our church had made, this person was of the same generation that called me out for my white shoes after Labor Day.) I held my breath, thinking to myself that this could be the moment that rips everything apart. This could ruin everything we had been working towards.

The room became silent, and all eyes turned toward Robert. I felt my heart begin to drop when he began: "This is asinine. I don't even know why we are debating this."

I could see my hopes and dreams being dashed to pieces as he continued:

> Many years ago, back in 1948, there was a young seminarian named Marty. Every week, members of our church would pick up Marty from Crozer Theological Seminary. Marty was a student there who would help our members minister to sailors at the shipyard who were transitioning back to civilian life. At the time, we were an all-White congregation and Marty was a Black man. Back in those days, this combination really turned heads, but it never once fazed our members. One night, we invited Marty out to dinner with us, and he obliged. When we got to the restaurant, Marty lingered outside. He had never had a meal in a White establishment before. We reassured him that if anybody had issues with it they would have to deal with the rest of us. He joined us at dinner, and we spent the night telling stories and laughing as we enjoyed each other's company. Marty was our friend, and we never once let society get in the way of how we felt about him. After Marty graduated, he moved on to much bigger things, and he went by a different name – a name you all may recognize – Rev. Dr. Martin Luther King, Jr. If Marty were here today, I know he would fight for the underdog just like we all had so many years ago. Our church has never been afraid of doing the right thing and we should continue to do that today.

The room burst into cheers and applause as Robert finished his speech. I had doubted him, but he surprised us all and affirmed something that I had long believed. This was not a matter of conservative or liberal, this was a matter of basic human rights. My husband and I both fought for Black rights in our youth; Larry even went to jail a few times while protesting. We both fought for women's rights as I challenged the system to become a female pastor, something that many people still do not approve of today. This was our fight now, and I made a promise to myself that I would fight for the good of all people until the day I die.

9

The Decision

After Robert's inspiring speech, I decided it was the right moment to take the vote. If that speech could not move this congregation to vote yes, then nothing would. We passed a basket around the room as each member deposited their ballot. The clock seemed to stop; every tic of the second hand echoed in my brain as I waited for all the votes to be collected. Finally, the basket made its way back to me.

Hopes were high, but even one "no" vote would defeat this motion. We had all agreed the vote must be unanimous, adhering to the policy at the time for becoming a welcoming and affirming Baptist Church. We counted every vote, one by one. I would take the paper out, unfold it, and show it to the members gathered around the room. Each time I opened a vote they screamed "yes," and with each passing "yes" my stress got worse.

Then, there it was. The last ballot. It was sitting at the bottom of the basket waiting for me to pick it up. Logically I knew that it would most likely be a "yes," but logic is never a guarantee, and frankly, has never been my strong suit. What if this was the one vote that would bring all our hopes tumbling down? Could this be some sort of cruel trick of fate? My heart was beating so fast I felt as if it would burst out of my chest.

I picked up that tiny piece of paper, knowing this small note would determine the future of Drexel Hill Baptist Church. I clenched my teeth, not wanting to show any emotion, and unfolded the paper in slow motion. I had to close my eyes, as I could not even bring myself to look at it. I held it up to the assembly. And then…silence.

There was not a sound. I opened my eyes, still holding the paper open to the multitude before me. I looked around and saw the big eyes of all one hundred members in the room. From the looks and hush of the crowd, I was certain it was the crushing blow. My heart almost stopped at that moment, just before I heard someone scream, "IT'S A YES!"

This was it. A message from God. This was the moment that would change the course of all our lives. There was no turning back. The room erupted as we all celebrated the incredible decision we had just made, and the impact it would have on our local and global community. I looked around and saw what I knew the church was and is meant to be: people from all walks of life coming together in unity to acknowledge and celebrate all of our differences.

Larry and I walked over to the door to lead the group out of our meeting room. On his way out, Larry grabbed the Christian flag out of the stand by the entrance. I had prepared for such an occasion and unrolled a rainbow flag. We affixed the rainbow flag to another flagpole, and together marched with the two flags side by side. We filed out of the front door of the church with our entire congregation in a grand parade. There would be no more hiding in the shadows. Our church was located on one of the busiest streets in our town. We proudly strode up and down the block in front of our church, showing our entire neighborhood that we were going to fight for the LGBTQ+ community.

Once I knew our congregation was on board with this new direction, I began consciously supporting the homosexuals in my congregation. I often accompanied them to gatherings that celebrated them as people. We stood in solidarity and protest against those spewing hate outside the Equality Forum's Civil Rights Summit; we had a booth to promote our church and ministry at the annual Gay Pride Festival; we even entered a float in the Pride Parade each year, which won awards every time. Once, while at a Gay Pride Festival in Philadelphia, a protestor approached me and started yelling in my ear with a megaphone, "Gay lover." I responded, "Yes, absolutely. I am a gay lover. I want to celebrate who they are and what wonderful gifts they are to the world." I do not think that was the response they quite expected.

10

Stop the Hurt

Let me tell you about one event that occurred shortly after we took that momentous vote, which became one of my most life-changing days; a day that turned from beauty to pain in the blink of an eye.

One day as I walked into a huge sanctuary on the University of Pennsylvania campus in Philadelphia, I was appreciating God and thanking God for the beautiful spring day before me. The weather that day was perfect, with budding trees gently swaying over the backdrop of a clear, blue sky. Upon entering the church, the stained-glass windows were radiant with glorious light. I was there attending a gathering for the LGBTQ+ faith community and their allies. My heart brimmed with hope for our church's new direction.

As I sat down in one of the pews, I felt such remarkable joy as I observed so many happy Christians. The place was a mix of gay couples, lesbian couples, heterosexual couples, transsexuals, Whites, Blacks, Asians, Indians, male, female, young, old – a beautiful mosaic of worshipers gathered together to love God and each other. It touched my soul so deeply to see this amazing diversity. I thought to myself, "Wow. This is truly God's Kingdom. This is how God's family should look, people of all different sizes, shapes, proclivities, and ethnicities." I knew this had to delight God, seeing people from all walks of life gathered in unity and worship.

Troy Perry, the founder of the Metropolitan Community Church, was speaking that day about the unity of all God's children. I know God loves and blesses unity. I could feel the Holy Spirit move among us as we celebrated this. The experience was genuinely ethereal. The worship and music felt like heaven on earth.

As the morning sessions wrapped up, I really did not want to leave to go for a lunch break. I wanted to bask in this magnificent moment and the presence of God. But I also knew I needed to eat! I walked out to the street directly in front of the church looking for food options nearby. Immediately, I encountered a new group of people that depicted a completely opposite side of humanity, a very ugly side. There were protesters spewing hatred in every direction at people they did not even know. Some held signs with hideous messages that blocked my view. They read, "God hates fags," "You are an abomination," "God hates you," and other vile messages that, in my mind, did not reflect the loving God I worship and serve. It felt like I had dropped from paradise right into a war zone. They rushed at me yelling horrible, unfathomable things. Megaphones magnified the sound of strangers shouting, "God hates you. God hates you." I was shocked that people were so filled with venom and loathing. When I realized they were doing it in God's name, I almost vomited.

In my world and my faith, God is not a hater. My God is love. I have given my entire life to help people feel loved by God. Those people representing and using God's name in such a violent and pejorative way were the opposite of love. I stood frozen in absolute disbelief. It hit me so hard. I am generally not an outwardly emotional person, but all I could do at that moment was cry. I have experienced protestors before, but this sudden onslaught of loathing crushed me like a boulder. It might have been the dichotomy of the situation in going from love to hatred so quickly, but whatever it was, I could not control my tears, streaming like a river down my cheeks. I cried all through lunch. I cried for the hatred that the LGBTQ+ community endures. I cried for what they experience daily. I cried for those that are told God hates them for who they are. I now had an insight into what my LGBTQ+ friends lived. No wonder so many have turned away from God. Who would want anything to do with a God that created them as different, then hated them for that exact difference?

I cried for myself, too, because it was so hurtful to have someone scream at me, "God hates you." I cried because my God, whose Word I live by and preach, was being represented in such a horrific way. If anyone believed what these supercilious people were alleging, that God hated them for being their authentic selves, they would most certainly turn away from God, the very one who loves them most. I knew logically this was just a group of self-righteous, misguided people, but it still hurt. What I did not understand was why it hurt me so deeply.

At that moment, I suddenly felt more compassion than I ever did before for those who were regularly targets of such horrific attacks. My heart ached, and still does today, to think of them subjected to such harsh, loveless barrages every single day. What I experienced in a brief five minute encounter, they experience all the time. The entire scene was unbelievably heartbreaking and so unnecessary, and as ungod-like as I had ever experienced. It had to tarnish the perception of Christianity in the mind of anyone who witnessed the altercation.

I returned to the gathering after lunch, looking like I had been crying for a solid hour, which I had. Surely I could stop and control myself, now that I was back in the safety of that incredible place of sanctuary. The Philadelphia Gay Men's Chorus was singing. I listened, still crying and praying for each one of them. The Holy Spirit had put a strong message inside of me that I could no longer ignore. God was clearly showing me a path.

The road laid before me was quite simple; I needed to stop the hurt. My crying would stop, but the pain I experienced that dreadful day would remain deep in my soul. At what point did it become acceptable to be malicious in the name of Christ? This world is indeed filled with many gray tones; it is not simply black and white. I understand that many do not agree with my views and beliefs about homosexuality. However, I do hope and pray that everyone can agree that loathing and violence are not what God teaches us or condones. And so, I am asking each of you reading this book to please help me stop the hate and stop the hurt.

11

Fusion or Confusion

After a few years of pointed outreach to the LGBTQ+ community, God eventually gave me the vision to start a church in downtown Philadelphia where the LGBTQ+ community could experience the love of Christ and be able to serve God within the church context. When God asked me to do it, the calling was so strong that I knew I had to follow through, despite the controversy that might ensue. Six hundred American Baptist Churches had already left the denomination over this issue. My heart aches for what they have gone through by following their true calling to exhibit the inclusive love of God.

When *The Philadelphia Inquirer* (a local newspaper in Philadelphia) printed the story that I was starting a gay Baptist Church, I went to a minister in our denomination for counsel and confessed, "I still don't know whether it is a sin or not, but I know God wants me to do this." Shockingly enough, the Drexel Hill Baptist Church, as well as the local American Baptist leadership, were supportive because they were struggling with the same issue. Of course, the church lost many members over this controversy because they did not understand the desperate need for this kind of healing ministry.

Our goal in planting our new church, called Fusion, was to create a safe place for everyone. Our brochure stated that "we have a particular concern that the Christian Church has effectively excluded individuals who are openly gay, lesbian, transsexual, and transgendered." We were different. We believed God's love is for all people. God loves ALL creation. We wanted that to be absolutely clear in everything we preached, printed, or portrayed.

In 2001, we began making plans to start "the first gay Baptist Church in the country," as the headlines in the newspaper read. An advanced special team from the Drexel Hill Baptist Church approached a church in downtown Philadelphia about the possibility of sharing their building with us and our new church, Fusion. It just so happened that at the same time, an anonymous anti-gay letter was circulating through their congregation. We were notified of the letter, which caused us to rethink our plan. Dividing other congregations over this matter was never our goal, so we withdrew our request. It did not take long to find another venue. Soon we began meeting in the beautiful sanctuary of the Lutheran Church of the Holy Communion. We were so grateful for their wonderful hospitality. We wanted desperately for the gay community to know that they are loved just as they are, just as God made them to be. The traditional high gothic style of the church surrounded our fledgling congregation with all the pomp and ceremony of church, reminding all that they were in the presence of God and surrounded by the love of God. Those who had been so hurt by the church needed the visual cues and prompts to reassure them of God's presence and love.

I believe strongly that when you do not allow people to be their true selves, they can never really feel loved because they fear that if they were authentic, they would be cut off from love. Unfortunately, this is a real anxiety that my experience has confirmed, which has spread far outside the church's doors. One of my co-founders at Fusion, a long-time organist at Drexel Hill Baptist Church who is gay, put it succinctly, "Until Fusion, Center City did not have any churches designated for gay people who have grown up with Bible-based church backgrounds. Many of them have suffered immeasurable amounts of damage at the hands of their churches. This is a church specifically for them." I was proud that we had begun the healing process for these marginalized and tortured souls.

Fusion was an incredible training ground. After worship each Sunday evening, I would invite anyone who had specific needs or concerns to come up to the front of the church and receive prayer. Never before had I experienced such pain and hurt. Yet in the midst of this incredible sadness and heartache, I witnessed the immense love and beauty buried deep in each of these precious people. Each time I prayed with an individual, I could feel the shame melting away, replaced by God's love and reassurance that this person was, indeed, a child of God.

The more we reached into the LGBTQ+ community, the more I became conscious of the breadth of devastation this group had suffered. I saw so many lives rejected by the church and even by their families; so many people loving God and wanting to serve God, yet not welcome to do so by the church. Devoted Christians who had been part of a church for years were discovered to be gay and shunned. Many others knew that they would be asked to leave if anyone found out, so in order to be accepted they lived a lie.

Launching Fusion resulted in many people coming to know me as a supporter for the LGBTQ+ community. As word on the street spread, they started to seek me out for counsel. I was filled with joy when I began to experience the charm, gentleness, and sensitivity common in the LGBTQ+ community. A little more drama perhaps than I was accustomed to, but I was always treated with genuine kindness and respect. Conversely, I was shocked by the outrage and hatred I experienced from many "church-going" heterosexuals.

An article was written in an Evangelical newsletter about Fusion called, "Fusion or Confusion." The article claimed that I "was confused as to the will of God." Amidst the controversy, I did not stop preaching at Fusion or Drexel Hill Baptist Church. I continued to help both my congregations come to know Jesus Christ as their Lord and personal Savior and become followers of Christ. I kept asking myself, "How could this be a bad thing?" I was sure this is what Jesus wanted all believers to do when he issued the "Great Commission," as told at the end of Matthew's gospel.

Shortly after starting Fusion, I was invited to be a guest on a radio station in Philadelphia to discuss our newly formed church and my views on homosexuality in the church. I was so excited about the opportunity to tell my story to eager listeners. I was not informed that they had also invited another minister with opposing views. The other minister pulled up in a black stretch limousine accompanied by two bodyguards. I tried to hide how shaken I was.

I knew immediately it was going to be an interesting encounter. The DJs were truly kind and loving, seeking to make me comfortable. My husband Larry waited in a separate room where he was able to watch me through the glass window. It was a difficult interview for me because, believe it or not, I disdain conflict. Yet God was working through me during the entire interaction; I remained calm, preaching love and forgiveness for ignorance.

Just as I was launching into my "Love Thy Neighbor" speech, I looked through the glass into the waiting room, and to my horror I saw my husband Larry pushing one of the bodyguards up against the wall in a very physical confrontation. I was trying to preach love and forgiveness, and there was Larry getting into a brawl. He was obviously not taking the high road, but I had to laugh when I saw just how much passion he had for me and my cause. He was normally the calm one! Apparently, while I was on the air, these bodyguards decided they were "soul guards" as well. They were emphatically telling Larry that he must convince me to quit this ridiculous quest and not be cast into hell. I do appreciate their concern for my soul, but my soul is safely in God's loving hands.

These bodyguards were not the only people convinced of my eternal destination if I continued this battle. Fred Phelps, pastor of the Westboro Baptist Church, in Topeka, Kansas, known for his protests against homosexuals (often at their funerals), called me "the whore of Babylon." It was unbelievably difficult for me to realize that people now hated me, people who did not even know me. People had always loved and respected me. Suddenly, I was actually getting hate mail and death threats. Most of the mail was anonymous, but some was from fellow Christians and colleagues imploring me to change my mind. Several inquired, "Jeri, I know you're a Christian, so what are you doing? Aren't you listening to God?" I would reply, "Yes, I AM listening." I would die before I went against what God has called me to do. I know God intimately; I talk to God all the time; I spend hours and hours each day reading scripture and devotions, praying, talking to, and, most importantly, listening to God. I know God's voice.

During this visceral struggle, I explained my plight to some of my seminary professors, seeking their guidance and counsel. I asked them to explain the "clobber passages" and their interpretation to me. These passages are the few instances in the Bible (about six in all) that reference the consequences of homosexuality. Surprisingly, these respected theologians admitted they were struggling as well. As we studied and prayed about it, the Holy Spirit led each of us to the same conclusion, which contradicted what we all had been taught from our childhood. Even with this shared consensus, I still struggled with what we should do to bring about change. I knew these dedicated teachers would likely be fired or lose their funding from conservative churches if their new perspectives were to become public. Coming out (so to speak) as an advocate for the LGBTQ+ community was not an option for any of them. I suggested we submit an article to the *Philadelphia Inquirer* where all the seminary professors in the area who had changed their minds would "come out" as LGBTQ+ allies. This produced a little anxiety in them, to say the least, which was never my intention. I love my seminary and my professors. I never want to do or suggest anything that would create division. It became clear that I had to continue the battle without their public support.

God was very busy transforming people's hearts and minds during our time with Fusion. We offered courses and seminars on the clobber passages. We had weekly prayer meetings, fellowship times, and worship. Additionally, we planned events that brought the Drexel Hill Baptist Church and the Fusion families together. Though they were two separate congregations and campuses, we wanted to promote unity by bringing the groups together.

After five years in downtown Philadelphia, Fusion and Drexel Hill Baptist Church merged and became one loving church. God had merged our hearts and minds, and now our congregations. Everyone wanted to worship and be together. Bible study and prayer cultivated lasting relationships in one place, with God and with each other. It was a beautiful experience.

A single friendship with a person unlike oneself, whether that person be of a different sexual orientation, race, religion, or the like, can change one's view completely. I always said just one impactful woman minister could change the heart and attitudes of many in a male-only clergy. It was time to expand that theory.

12

Whose Agenda is This

In the mid-1990s, my husband Larry and I attended a Christian conference in Virginia. It began as a beautifully sacred and loving gathering; we were thrilled to be a part of it. These types of symposia always renewed us, spiritually, and refreshed us, physically. Additionally, a break from the regular routine and a change of scenery were a welcome pause in our hectic lives. As we were enjoying the wonderful teachings, music, and fellowship, I kept thinking that we should have brought some of our church family to participate in this fabulous event. What a treat it would be for them experience this uplifting and educational forum.

On the second day, the leaders of the conference began addressing what they proudly labeled "The Homosexual Agenda," which included reiterating the standard Bible-based family values. It was quite obvious that, in their minds, these values clearly did not include family members who were openly gay. They were certain that homosexuals had a negative agenda of their own to ruin the American family. They were convinced that gays were scheming to undermine the entire moral character of this country.

The dichotomy of emphasizing loving God and each other to emphasizing exclusion and hatred was utterly mind boggling. How could these leaders, who proclaim to be stewards of God's love here on earth, seem so far from possessing that love? Larry and I were thoroughly disgusted by the hypocrisy being demonstrated. I could not help but pray, "Oh merciful God, thank you for keeping me from bringing my church family here." Some of my dear, sweet, LGBTQ+ congregation would have been so hurt, once again being branded as beyond the love of God by those called to love even their enemies.

13

A Seminary for All

Fusion was well into its third year; tremendous things were happening. The LGBTQ+ community fully trusted us now, and more hearts were turning back to the Almighty. But not everything was wonderful. One of the most disappointing events in my pastoral career centered around twelve amazing young LGBTQ+ people with such incredible potential, ready to give their entire lives to serving God. Each of them wanted to go to seminary to prepare for ministry. They had felt God call them to ministry, but needed the proper training and education to be obedient to that call. Excited to guide them on this path, I took them to an open house at the Baptist seminary nearby to learn all about the programs, the requirements, and the school itself.

We arrived in our big church bus, which was a repainted school bus with a rainbow flag on the side (rather funny now, looking back). My prospective students were ecstatic with the possibility of their future ministry and felt compelled to apply for seminary as soon as possible. Obedience to God's call was first and foremost in their minds. Minor issues, such as tuition costs, application hurdles, and current job responsibilities, never got in their way, as they knew those things would fall into place in God's time.

Most of these precious students will not know this, unless they are reading these words, but I spoke privately to the admissions director that day. I did not want to make a big show, but I was overjoyed to be bringing twelve new students to the seminary from our small congregation. There were a few members of Fusion already enrolled in seminary, some even in their last year. I thought the director, too, would be thrilled to be recruiting this group of new students, so I was downright confused by his response. He informed me, gently albeit emphatically, that "this was not the place for them." Though I would never let him see it, I was shaken to my very core, heartbroken that this seminary that I have supported for years had turned their back on some of God's most obedient children. I struggled to hold back my tears the entire ride home on that beautiful rainbow bus. When I finally reached the solitude and sanctity of my office back at church, I could no longer contain myself. I was so hurt that I cried out to God, "This is so wrong. People want to give their whole lives to You to serve You, and they are not welcome to even be trained in ministry? We know the amazing things the first twelve disciples of Yours did. We can only imagine the impact twelve more can have in this century."

I cried and prayed for weeks, waiting for God to show me where these devoted disciples should turn for the necessary ministerial training. Finally, God spoke to me, "You know you need to start a seminary." Thus came the birth of the John Stevenson Hall School of Ministry, with a full seminary curriculum, including Old Testament studies, New Testament studies, Hebrew and Greek language classes, theological colloquium, pastoral care training, systematic theology, church history, preaching, worship, and all the other usual ministry courses. We had a registrar, syllabi, books, grades, and even highly qualified professors from the local seminary. Our seminary successfully ran for over eight years.

In 2013, my husband, who was the primary professor, passed away suddenly and unexpectedly. I was not able to handle the demands of running the seminary and the fulltime ministry at the church, so classes ceased. Many of our treasured students have since transferred to mainline seminaries. Although we never sought the formal accreditation process, some of our students did receive transfer credits for the courses they took at our seminary. The John Stevenson Hall Seminary remains one of my proudest accomplishments.

14

Misplaced Intentions

I love being an American Baptist. It has given me the freedom to do what God has called me to do and be. There are two tenets of the faith that have strong bearing on this freedom: soul liberty and freedom of conscience. Soul liberty means that each person in the church is entitled to discern what their own soul dictates is right, based on that individual's relationship with and responsibility to God. This principle of soul liberty has given me the autonomy to come to my own understanding of what God is calling me to do as a pastor and what we should do as a congregation. Freedom of conscience, which simply allows us to have differing views, thoughts, or interpretations of God and scripture, affords American Baptists a way to agree to disagree, and to respect other people's own relationship with Christ. We respect each other's individual conclusions on how to best serve God and put our faith into practice.

Traditionally, the Christian Church, as a whole, is not a warm, welcoming, or affirming place for the LGBTQ+ community. While some churches or denominations do welcome everyone, when it comes time for further involvement in leadership with the church, they cut off the affirming part. Individuals judged to be living outside God's "acceptable" ways are not permitted to teach Sunday school, lead small study groups, lead worship, or serve on church boards or committees.

The phrase most often used is "love the sinner, hate the sin." On the surface, this seems to be a beautiful sentiment. But at a deeper level, it is not comforting and certainly not very respectful or caring to the people to whom it is directed (as I experienced firsthand in seminary). Why is homosexuality the only sin that seems to fall under this category? What about all the sins the Bible calls out, such as gluttony, greed, pride, and envy? Saying "homosexuality is a sin, but you love homosexuals anyway" is not enough. It is time to honestly and prayerfully look at what God considers sin in our own lives and stop judging the lives and actions of others, especially those we do not even know.

When I first entered the ministry, I truly did not believe women belonged in pastoral ministry, based on what I had been taught my entire life. I was happy to be involved in Christian education or any of the other traditional roles for women in the church. I had absolutely no desire to be, or fight to be, a senior pastor. I tried everything in my power to ignore God's call to become a pastor because I thought having a woman leading a church was not appropriate. On a deep level, I knew I was called by God into ministry, but I thought the calling was limited to Christian education or some other acceptable role for a female. However, that all changed in a big way when I began to preach. The day I delivered my first sermon as an intern, I knew change was on the horizon. The Holy Spirit was flowing through me, and there was nothing I could do to stop it. I had little choice in the matter because I knew that God was pushing me beyond my upbringing and my comfort level. In obedience, I followed the path.

I genuinely felt God had called me to preach, but I struggled to accept it because I still did not believe women belonged in the front of the church. My interpretation of the Scripture at the time was that it might be sinful to take such an authoritative role in the church as a woman, my own preference being to see a big, strong man in the pulpit. In retrospect, I cannot believe I ever felt that way. The phrase "love the sinner, but hate the sin" was commonly used then by those against women in the ministry, implying I was committing a sin by being a female pastor. I continued to wrestle with the call, studying the Scriptures diligently, finally writing my doctoral dissertation on women in ministry. After studying biblical Greek and Hebrew extensively, carefully examining the context in which the Scriptures were written and the people whom the writers were addressing at the time, I came to a very different conclusion about women in ministry. I knew without a doubt that God had called me to do God's work, just as God has called countless other women into ministry. Furthermore, it was not a sin. I can see so clearly now that God created me to be a pastor of a church.

Now it was time to stand up to the old ways of thinking again, this time taking on those who used this phrase against the LGBTQ+ community.

15

An Amazing Child of God

I always knew there was something unique about my son John. I have three sons, but John was just always so different, in a very delightful way. When he was three or four years old, I went into his room late one night to check on him, expecting him to be sound asleep in his bed. Instead, I found him on his knees by his bed with his arms stretched upward praying, "Jesus, I want to go home." This was startling, to say the least. Why would a preschooler be asking the Lord to take him home? Part of me started to wonder if he might die at a young age. Yet, I knew if God gave him the chance, John would grandly affect the world. I was right.

His twin brother James played with trucks and a work bench as a child, while John played with Barbie dolls and Calico Critters. He even liked playing with Ken. He wanted everything Barbie, including Barbie's Dream House. My father-in-law kept insisting we "get him some trucks," and I kept thinking, "but he doesn't

LIKE trucks, and I can't force him to play with them when he is obviously happier playing with Barbies." I suppose his sexual orientation should have been undeniably evident to us, but we never gave it a second thought. John was just different, and we loved him just the way he was.

Always opting for more artistic avenues, he learned how to play the piano at a young age. When he was thirteen, he started putting music to my sermons. It was uncanny how he could hear my sermon once and immediately play an interpretation of it on the piano. It was obvious to me that the Holy Spirit was upon him. He never took notes about what I said, he just started playing the most amazing music that transformed my sermon into a beautiful song. "How can he be a Christian if he is gay?" people would often ponder. My response was always the same, "How could he NOT be a Christian when it is so obvious that he has the Holy Spirit working through him?" We were all watching a truly undeniable miracle.

At the age of fifteen, John came to Larry and me in our living room at the parsonage and announced, matter-of-factly, that he was gay.

I remember asking him, "Are you sure? When you look at a girl you don't get butterflies, but when you look at a guy, you do?" He assured me he only got butterflies looking at guys! By the time he came out, I had been ministering at Fusion for quite a while. It was a beautiful gift that God had so miraculously prepared my husband and me to deal with John's announcement in a loving accepting manner, though we were a bit surprised and did have questions. If God had not so carefully, gently, and lovingly prepared us for this unforeseen moment, it could have been disastrous in many ways. John's sexuality would have been so clearly unacceptable and shaming to the church and to us that he would have never come out. John would never do anything to hurt God's kingdom here on earth, and he certainly would not have done anything to damage his parents' reputation or ministry. More importantly, had he not been able to openly admit he was gay and live authentically, he would definitely not be the amazing, loving, creative person he is now.

It is common practice for local church leadership to approach ministers whose children exhibit "un-biblical" behavior, instructing them to keep their children "under control" or be ousted from the church. Over the years, our church had become so loving and accepting, I was extremely glad he felt comfortable enough to come out to Larry, me, and the church congregation at such a young age. John never had self-esteem issues because we never made him feel like he was anything less than an amazing child of God. When children feel unconditionally loved and accepted by their parents, peers, and especially by God, they thrive and are able to cultivate the wonderful gifts and talents God gave them.

I admit there was a part of me that thought, "Did I make him gay?" But I knew enough at that point to realize that no parent makes their children gay, straight, or whatever. It was hard at first to turn a deaf ear to all the accusations that I was somehow responsible for him being homosexual. People kept saying, "If you hadn't been so into helping gays and letting John hang around them, your son would have turned out straight." Really? My other two sons grew up in the same house, around all the same people, and they are not gay. Our sexuality is not something learned, it is inherent in our psyche from the moment we are born.

16

Go Sleep with the Boys

As a result of the many years I spent developing close relationships with people in the gay community, I was much more in tune with some of John's struggles. I remember one particular situation when we were shopping at a department store. John was humorously steering me away from clothes that were less than flattering. We were laughing and having so much fun. He is a terrific fashion consultant and has an eye for what would be stylish and suitable for me. He always told me that, if left to my own devices in a clothing store, I would be a "hot mess." We were in a private dressing room, and I was trying on some of the items John meticulously picked out for me. Suddenly, a salesclerk angrily knocked on the dressing room door. She said rather curtly, "I am sorry, but HE needs to leave." I remember feeling so hurt, mostly for John. I responded with equal curtness, "He's gay and is helping me pick out my clothes." Then, rhetorically I continued under my breath, "I can't believe your store has not thought about this kind of situation before. How do you handle people who happen to be intersex or transgender?"

A similar disquieting situation arose during a youth group retreat in the mountains of Pennsylvania. When we arrived at the retreat center, John wanted to sleep in the room with the girls, as he usually did. I had no problem with this arrangement because after all, he is gay. The girls always loved having him bunk with them, and that is where he was most comfortable. In addition, I was staying in the girls' room, so they all would be under the watchful eye of Pastor and Mom. The head of the retreat house heard about the situation, came into the girls' room, and forcibly made John leave. I explained to the retreat house head, "He is my son, and he is gay. I am the chaperone for this group. I can assure you there is no danger of any shenanigans happening here." He refused to allow John to sleep in the same room with the girls, insisting he sleep with the boys (ironic, really). John ended up sneaking back to sleep in the girls' room with us anyway.

What I want people to understand from these stories is that life is just not that simple anymore. It is possible that some of the other youth on our retreats were gay, both boys and girls. We cannot know for certain, unless they have come out publicly. Our youth leadership tried to take this into account on these trips, but it was not always cut-and-dried. During another youth trip, two girl-crazy young boys (or so we thought) were placed in a room farthest from the girls' cabin to ensure they would not sneak out to "visit" the girls in the middle of the night. I found out years later they were a gay couple. Imagine my surprise. I had no idea! The point is, we just do not know anymore. But the more we shame and hurt people, like my son, for being who God made them to be, the more we stifle the beauty within each one of them.

Friends, we must shift our thinking on this issue, especially with the teenage population. If we do not instill trust and acceptance in them at an early age, they will likely conceal their sexual orientation, and we may push them farther from God rather than closer.

17

The Boy in the Closet

Another encounter, which took place at our Fusion campus, touched me deeply. As I mentioned before, after each service at Fusion, I invited anyone who felt they needed extra prayers to come up to the altar. A young man who had never attended Fusion before walked up and stood in front of me. He stood poised and composed, appearing very self-assured. I quickly found out looks are deceiving.

As I prayed over him, my hand on his shoulder, I began to feel overwhelmingly claustrophobic. It was such a strong feeling that I said out loud, "Did you live in a small space? I am getting a strong closed-in feeling." His demeanor took an abrupt turn, as his confidence melted away, and he began to sob uncontrollably. I asked the others who had come up for prayer if they would give us a moment so that this young man could speak to me with some degree of privacy. After he calmed down, he told me that when he was a teenager, he confessed to his father that he was gay. His father responded, "Okay, if you are going to continue being gay you have to live in the closet." His father meant this literally. This young man was forced to stay in a closet in his house. He would come home from school and go directly to the closet where he ate and slept. No wonder he was having a difficult time with his past and constantly feeling unworthy, for which he was obviously trying to overcompensate with his somewhat cocky attitude. Sadly, there were, and still are, so many people being treated just as inhumanely, who have built up these facades to hide their fears and hurts.

The irony of this story was not lost on me. This young man was literally and figuratively forced to stay in his closet, against his will, and made to feel like he deserved less than everyone else because of his sexuality. How many others like him are forced to stay in the closet for fear they would be treated just as horribly as this sweet, young boy?

This young man continued attending Fusion, where he was totally accepted and loved, and eventually became a devout Christian. He went on to get his master's in social work and is thriving in his community, helping others who face this same condemnation. When I saw how this man flourished when treated with respect, love, and approval, it strengthened my conviction to continue helping the LGBTQ+ community, despite death threats and hate mail that piled up in my mailbox daily. The need was, and is, so great that it must outweigh the fears of standing up to the injustice and inequality.

18

A Price to Pay

It is often difficult to follow what God has called me to do because it seems to always involve living counter-culturally. Larry and I have lost many dear members of our congregation because they strongly disagreed with our accepting attitudes. We have also lost many potential members of our congregation, as they realize who we are and the values for which we stand.

One specific family, who were genuinely caring and loving people, began attending our church on a regular basis. They were moved by our sermons, and Larry and I both felt they would be a wonderful altruistic addition to our church family. I was heartbroken when they took me aside one Sunday after service and inquired, "We love you and Larry, and your sermons always touch us on a deep level. However, we are concerned with the members who are homosexual. Do you condone those who hold hands during your services?"

I was bewildered by their question because they had always seemed so tolerant and non-judgmental. I quickly responded, "Well of course, why wouldn't I? There is nothing wrong with people who love each other holding hands. It shouldn't matter whose hand someone holds, should it?" They heartily disagreed and never came back to church. Needless to say, my views and beliefs are not always the most popular, but they come from years of listening to God. I am not in ministry to win any popularity contests. I intend to be obedient to God's call and direction, wherever that leads.

Despite the hurdles we endured, ours is a story of great victory. Not victory as a traditional church; we are FAR from traditional. I wish I could make the claim that our church grew steadily because our open, welcoming, and embracing stance drew many to join with us. That was not the case. We dropped to roughly sixty members, maybe even less than that at one point.

Growing a welcoming and affirming church in a suburban community, where the last thing on people's minds is LGBTQ+ rights and acceptance of diversity, turned out to be more challenging than I realized. Uh-oh, did I say that out loud? Our church was strong, alive, and vibrant, but small in numbers. Additionally, we were maintaining a 22,000 square foot colonial building that was aging and in need of some substantial repairs. Those of us who lived through the process of becoming "welcoming and affirming" had grown tremendously in character, love, Biblical knowledge, and spirituality. Now we were more dependent upon Christ than ever. We became a different church altogether. But we still had a large, traditional structure to support, and it was draining our spirits as well as our funds.

We, as a congregation, had been totally transformed. Our music, which had been traditional organ and choir before, was now a full praise band with drums, electric guitar, keyboards, and vocals.

We changed our governing structure from boards and committees to elders, deacons, and teams, based on biblical models. Our mission statement became, "We will do whatever it takes to bring people into God's Kingdom." We even resolved to be a uniquely nonjudgmental body of Christ, which, as can be expected, is an ongoing process for us individually and corporately. Our focus moved away from activities and programs toward worship and prayer. People even lifted their hands in praise to their God, which as Baptists was unprecedented. Devotional life and Bible study were strongly emphasized. A total concentration on our individual and corporate relationship with our Creator became the center of congregational life.

God had woven together a tapestry of truly diverse people: heterosexual, LGBTQ+, rich, poor, old, young, Black, White, Hispanic, families of all conglomerations. We believed that THIS is how the body of Christ should look.

What happened next was astonishing. We realized that the church was the people, not the building. Our utility bills alone were running $18,000 a month, and our sanctuary was not even air conditioned in the summer. Surely we could be better stewards of God's money. So, we decided to go green, looking for a tiny sanctuary on plenty of land for farming and community supported agriculture, investigating solar and geothermal energy options, rain collection, composting, recycling, and any other environmentally sensitive avenue we could. We took a giant transforming step, changed the name of our church to The Green Church, and sold our building in Drexel Hill, which had been our congregation's home for more than forty years. We knew it was time.

The prospect of finding a new building was daunting. During this time, Larry and I ran into a minister from another church. The minister had recently moved from an urban church to a rural church. We asked him what it was like. He explained that the church he was leading now was like a Hollywood theme park, in comparison. I responded, "Wow, I want THAT!" God and I always had a unique communion when I would visit Disney World. We have a timeshare there and have gone at least once or twice every year since our twins were three months old. That is definitely our family's happy place, so this man's description of his rural setting became my desire, but only if it fit with God's plan.

Shortly after this conversation, I had a dream which was so clear and real that, for a moment after waking, I was not certain what was real and what was not. In that dream I saw a house, a small house with a "C" on it, with a huge, beautiful, lacy willow tree in the expansive front yard. As I strolled under the willow tree in this dream, God spoke to my heart, saying, "Jeri, this is your happy place."

As soon as I got out of bed that morning, I called the church moderator and told her what I had seen and heard in that crazy dream. She exclaimed, "I know the house, I know the people who own the house. Let's go see it now." We went that morning. As we approached the property, I could hardly believe what I saw. It was the exact house in my dream, including the willow tree. It was God-given and perfect in every way for our situation. The "C" was mounted on the pool house, a "small house" behind the main house. It all sat on three acres of land.

God gave us a few more clues to let us know this was the place for us. The first was the bus. My husband said that if we ever moved, he would not ever park the rainbow bus out in the front. So, guess what? There was a pad made just for the bus behind the garage so it would not have to sit front-and-center, but could still be seen in the distance.

The second was the copper bell out by the pool. The homeowners had been trying to donate this immense bell to a church or civic organization for over thirty years, as they believed it would be more beneficial in that type of setting. While Larry and I were inquiring about possibly buying the house, the homeowners realized that our church should have the beautiful bell, and the house as well! They could not deny (and neither could we) that this was a God ordained fit. They were Christians who trusted in God's timing, so they patiently waited for us to finalize the sale of our former church building in Drexel Hill. Not only did they accommodate our time frame, but they sold us the property at an incredible price for that area. God's timing is always perfect.

A few years later after Larry had passed away, I was having a rough moment missing him terribly. In the midst of my loneliness and grief, my son Andrew came up from the pool and inquired, "Mommy, did you ever notice what the inscription is on the bell?" Honestly, I had never really looked at it before. I assumed it said God Bless America, or something of that sort. He convinced me to go look at it. I could not believe my eyes. It said, "The Lord defendeth the fatherless and the widow" [Psalm 146:9], both of which we now represented. We cried then laughed, and I remarked, "I should've read that before we moved in."

Our new house was an amazing home, where we hosted many congregational gatherings for prayer, study, and fellowship. But now we needed a space more conducive to Sunday morning worship, since the zoning restrictions did not allow worship gatherings on less than six acres. We went to the local park and thought it might work in nice weather. Our wonderful elders began looking through Eddie Bauer catalogues trying to find coats and boots, in case we had to worship outside in the winter. They were willing to go wherever God was leading us, even if that was out into the snow.

We went to firehouses and community buildings to investigate our options. One day my moderator and I drove by a tiny church building on eleven acres of land. There was a man, who looked like he might be the pastor, exiting the church and descending the steps to the parking lot. We slowly drove into the parking lot as he proceeded to get in his van and drive to what we discovered was the parsonage on the back of the property behind a grove of trees. We felt like stalkers as we watched and waited until he left the parsonage and returned to the sanctuary. You might think this was a bit unusual even for us, but we were desperately searching everywhere for the last piece of the puzzle, leaving no possible stone unturned.

As we approached the church stairs, the pastor greeted us, "Can I help you?" He was probably irritated that we were hovering, but he mustered a slight smile. "We're not really sure what we're doing," I replied, "but what is the story of this church? We bought a parsonage down the street and, at this point, we're not sure what God has in mind for us."

His smile grew in amazement. "Well, you're not going to believe this," he chuckled, "but let me show you the 'For Sale' sign in the trash area in the back of the church. We have been trying to sell for two years. We've had some rough negotiations, so we finally decided to take the sign down and we've been praying that whoever was supposed to have this property, God would just have to send them to our doorstep."

Because we were obedient and followed a strong message from God, as crazy as it felt, it all worked out beautifully and in God's perfect timing. We temporarily worshiped at Garrett-Williamson, a local nonprofit farm and educational facility, as we were searching for our new location. We remained there a total of about six months, until we were ready to move into this marvelous, little sanctuary. The next chapter in our transformational history had begun.

I shared this miraculous vision in my sermon during worship in June of 2012. We moved to the "C-House" in September and The Green Church on December 1, 2012. Sometimes God moves so fast, it makes my head spin. God is so amazing, so divine.

19

Vision for The Green Church

God gave me a vision for The Green Church of waterfalls, fountains, plants, gardens – truly a paradise on earth where hope is found, and where people can come to worship and experience the sheer beauty of God's creation. We were to be a church, not just of physical beauty, but where all people are down to earth, authentic, and real; a church where Jesus is the number one priority in every life, and all are fully committed to God and to each other.

A dream was placed in my heart for a church where the Sabbath is truly celebrated, where Sundays included donuts and bagels, fresh coffee and orange juice, then worship, fellowship, and breaking of bread. A place where, in the warmer months, Sunday includes church picnics with a beautiful array of foods, where we love and serve each other. There would have to be a barbeque and swimming pool, of course. We would spend the whole day together, swimming, eating good food, and celebrating all that God has done for us. In this place, we would dwell in love and fellowship with God and with each other.

God is so good to us. We now have a church house with a beautiful pool, and every Sunday we gather, eat, play, and celebrate. We even added a Tiki bar and a hot tub for more fun. In the winter months, we set up an ice-skating rink in the back of the house where we skate and have S'mores and hot chocolate by the fire pit. We watch movies and play games in the family room inside. Everyone contributes in some way. Everyone looks forward to Sundays, which should be a fabulous day that we look forward to all week long. I cannot wait for the day when my congregation exclaims, "Thank God It's Sunday!" I think most already do. The Lord's Day is the best day of the week.

My vision for us is this: love God so much, which we do, that when others see how extraordinarily joyful and peaceful we are, they will be drawn into the Kingdom of God just by knowing us. I imagine a church that grows its own fruits and vegetables. We are working as fast as we can seeking environmentally friendly ways to save God's creation. I dream of a campus that is so awesome that children, youth, and people of all ages will be yearning to come, pray, and enjoy fellowship together. That is happening. The children are dragging their parents to church instead of the other way around. The Green Church is not only welcoming and affirming, but embracing of ALL people. We are reaching out beyond ourselves to share the Gospel and the love of Christ.

We have become a church where we rejoice in the Lord and live life abundantly. This is a place where the welcome gifts are monogramed pool towels, mugs, and S'mores sticks. We want it to be a place of belonging. We are no longer a congregation, we are a FAMILY. We are diligently working on loving one another. We decided if we are really going to love one another, then we must spend some time together, which we happily do. We share our strengths and work on our weaknesses; we really are building relationships with each other on a very deep level.

I know that faith is supposed to be as natural as breathing. It should be a part of everything that we do. There are a lot of people who live several disconnected lives: go to church on Sunday, work on Monday, and then a party on Friday. They become different people at all those events, which is possible because these partitioned lives never intersect. I want each member of The Green Church to be authentic and real, in EVERY part of their lives – loving God and being the best that each can be for God. I love God with my entire heart, soul, strength, and mind, and so, of course, I want everyone to experience that, too. Our congregation has come to strongly believe that spending a lot of time together helps us grow together as a family of God. We sincerely love God and each other, and we want to serve God and God's creation.

We know God has great plans for us beyond anything that we could ask or imagine. Our gathering space is now at an arboretum that has 650 acres of fabulous landscaping, with gardens galore (including an edible garden and a butterfly garden), treehouses, and all the elegance and allure of nature you can imagine. We worship in a restored barn. It is a place where you can be swept away by the beauty of God's creation that surrounds you. It is perfect in fulfilling the vision for The Green Church in every way possible.

We offer a series of courses designed to cultivate and deepen our relationships with each other and with God. The first is a four-week course in loving self. People with self-esteem issues need a place where they can set goals and learn to love themselves so they can love others. Once people complete that course, they can join a second four-week course on loving God's creation. Here people are actively involved in gardening and farming, taking care of animals and crops, learning how to sustain God's creation. A third course in the series focuses on loving others. People participate in harvesting and giving away our crops to the less fortunate, and going to downtown Philadelphia to share food with the homeless, reaching out to "the least of these." The final course is on loving God, where we learn how to do devotions, Bible study, fast, and pray. The emphasis is to develop our individual relationship with God.

People who are interested in the environment, diversity, and being open to the LGBTQ+ community are welcome. We do not judge based on color, race, economic status, or sexual orientation. We embrace everyone. We know that God welcomes all of God's people, and God wants to be in a personal and intimate relationship with them.

We also offer a course on the clobber passages. As I explained earlier, the clobber passages are the passages in the Bible that are used to hurt other people and force conformity. They are too often quoted to make people feel "less than" and not welcome in God's Kingdom. We do not believe that homosexuality is a sin. The scriptures have been studied at length by myself and our congregation, as well as other theologians and scholars who agree with our interpretation. We concluded that each of these instances was addressing a specific culture and condition in that culture, primarily speaking against humiliation, control, and subordination of God's children, not acts of love between two consenting adults. If we accepted these passages the way they have traditionally been understood, then we would also have to accept slavery and the oppression of women, as well as give up cheeseburgers. We have studied the original Hebrew text. We have studied the original Greek text. We have dug deep to uncover the truth of what each means to us today. We have come to these conclusions from a position of knowledge, not lack thereof. Because we have studied, researched, and prayed for wisdom, God has opened our hearts and our minds.

Our church is not everyone's cup of tea. On the Myers Briggs scale, we are made up of mostly NTs (Intuitive plus Thinking) and NFs (Intuitive plus Feeling). We have a different way of thinking. We say to be a grain of sand amidst a billion other grains of sand is to be nothing. We want to make a difference in this world. We will do "whatever it takes" to accomplish our mission.

Every day I thank God for where God has brought us. Our victory is, and always will be, in love.

20

Still More to Go

In July of 2016, I found myself once again gathered with my church family and like-minded Christians at the Mazzoni Center, in Philadelphia, to oppose the anti-gay group from Westboro Baptist Church. They had announced their intention to gather at the corner of Eighth and Locust Streets to picket the Center, which largely focuses on trans-affirming programs and LGBTQ+ wellness and support. It serves as a lifeline for many in the community who have been ostracized by family and friends.

I was surprised when only four people from the Kansas-based church showed up, as more than 1,000 counter-protestors, including myself, formed a wall of love to block the array of hateful messages expected from the Westboro Baptist Church legion.

The few WBC protestors who were there dispersed after heavy police pressure, coupled with chants from the crowd to "go home," which overwhelmed them. They knew they were outnumbered and defeated by the passion for open-mindedness we demonstrated. The outpouring of empathy for the LGBTQ+ community was awe-inspiring. It was a day of love of which I was so honored to be a part.

Twenty-some years ago when I began this journey, this would have been a vastly different scene. The numbers would have been reversed, with our meager reserves trying to stand against their expansive army. So maybe, just maybe, we are beginning to understand and really trust that love conquers all. It is amazing to see the progress that has occurred over these many years; progress that is often missed when we stare into the face of hatred in 2020 and beyond. Unfortunately, the hatred continues, but love grows and conquers more and more with each passing day. I cannot believe how far we have come, and I cannot believe how far we still have to go.

21

Why Should I Have a Gay Son

To many people, having a gay son may seem like a burden or a struggle. I will not lie, there have been many challenges, with countless nights spent lying awake fearful that he was not safe outside the shelter of our home and church. I was scared John would be bullied while he was in school. When he was at work I was afraid he would be fired. When he moved out on his own I was even more terrified that he might even be killed. The homophobes in this world can come out of nowhere and attack when least expected. I was petrified that John would be caught off-guard at some point by one or more of these fanatics. But parents worry about their children, no matter what their sexual orientation is. That is what parents do.

Having a gay son has driven me to be even stronger in standing up to the bullies, and to demonstrate to him that I would do anything for him, just as I would for any of my children. It has also strengthened my resolve to fight for what I believe is right and to question what I have always been told. I have learned that nothing is just black and white; much in this world is gray and subject to individual interpretation. There can be many "right" answers to one question. But I think the most important thing it has taught me is how to be a more compassionate and loving person. Witnessing the prejudice and discrimination my son has faced since he came out was a lesson in just how cruel the world can be. I want to be a force of goodness and kindness to combat that cruelty. I will overcome evil with good (Rom 12:21).

I see my son in every person that has traveled on a rough road in life. I see him in every homeless person looking for a place to rest their head. I see him in every child being bullied at school. I see him in minorities in nearby communities who experience intolerance and discrimination. Each of these gentle souls lives in a constant state of feeling less than their middle-class, White peers for no other reason than their nationality, their socio-economic status, or the color of their skin.

Having a gay son has made me a better mom, a better person, a better neighbor, a better pastor, and a better Christian.

22

Apologies to the LGBTQ+ Community

I would be remiss if, in this book, I did not offer my sincerest apology for all the damage and hurt that I have witnessed inflicted on the LGBTQ+ community. From the bottom of my heart I apologize. I wish I could take away all the harm, suffering, and pain each of you have gone through.

I am sorry for any time you were made to feel "less than."

I am sorry for all the heartache you have endured.

I am sorry for words you heard that were cruel and demeaning.

I am sorry for any time someone looked at you with disdain.

I am sorry for every time someone judged you for being you.

I am sorry for any time you felt you could not be yourself for fear of rejection or injury.

I am sorry for anytime someone did not ask about your significant other, and you felt awkward.

I am sorry for anytime you did not feel loved.

I am sorry for anytime someone made fun of you because you were different from them.

I am sorry for anytime people told you God did not love you.

I am sorry for anytime you felt excluded.

I am sorry for anytime you did not feel welcomed.

I am sorry for all the times you felt that if people knew who you really were, they would not love you.

I am sorry for anytime you thought God did not make you the way you were supposed to be.

I am sorry for people telling you that you are a sinner because you are LGBTQ+.

I am sorry for anytime someone told you that you needed to change.

I am sorry for those of you who felt the need to change from the beautiful, unique person God made you to be just to be accepted.

I am sorry for the conversations that took a turn for the worse when the person you were talking to realized you were LGBTQ+.

I am sorry for the times you were made to feel like an outsider, like you did not belong.

I am sorry for the times you were not allowed to love and serve in God's church.

I am sorry for all the times you were rejected in the home of God.

I am sorry for any time you were bullied for being yourself.

I am sorry for all the times you were unable to express your likes, dislikes, talents, and abilities because they were not gender appropriate.

I am sorry for anytime you felt the pain of rejection.

I am sorry for all the times Christians have called you an abomination.

I am sorry for all who have been brave enough to "come out" and then been rejected by and thrown out of their own families.

I am sorry for all the lives that were lost because they felt so alienated they took their own life.

I am sorry for those who have been beaten up and murdered for who God made them to be.

You are a child of God, loved by the Almighty, and created just as you are supposed to be in God's image. Please do not let anyone tell you otherwise.

Rev. Dr. Jeri E. Williams and her husband, Rev. Lawrence A. Williams

The three Williams boys – a long time ago!

The Williams family on vacation

Rev. Jeri Williams, her sister Nancy, and their dog, Babby

Rev. Jeri Williams (right) with (left to right) her sister Nancy, her grandmother, her brother Gary, and her mother

*Rev. Williams' grandfather, Rev. John Stevenson
Hall, preaching under a tree in Kaltungo*

*Rev. Williams' mother, in Kaltungo, grinding grain into
flour while babysitting a neighbor's child*

Rev. Williams' grandmother reading the Bible and teaching the Kaltungo women and their children

Rev. Williams' grandfather in his "office" working on the Bible translation

EVERYONE SHOULD HAVE A GAY SON

Rev. Williams' uncles (left) at the 1990 dedication of the John Stevenson Hall Memorial Church in Kaltungo

Rev. Williams greeting the multitude at the 2017 centennial celebration in Kaltungo

2008 Philadelphia Pride Parade – Fusion/Drexel Hill Baptist Church congregation

Everyone Should Have a Gay Son

2008 Philadelphia Pride Parade – Fusion/Drexel Hill Baptist Church float

2008 Philadelphia Pride Parade – Fusion/Drexel Hill Baptist Church parade participants

Rev. Dr. Jeri Williams at a 2016 protest in support of the Mazzoni Center in Philadelphia (The Mazzoni Center is dedicated to the health and wellness of the LGBTQ+ community)

The Williams' sons today

Section II
Stories of Transformation

These stories are written by individuals whose lives have been directly impacted by the work of Rev. Dr. Jeri Williams and The Green Church.

—1—

Rose's Story

I gleaned so much while collaborating with the Rev. Dr. Jeri Williams on this beautiful book. I know God works in truly miraculous ways, and I was reminded of God's grace in countless ways throughout this entire process.

Just as Jeri and I began talks about possibly working together on her book, my son Jim came out, not to me, but to a good friend of mine. I am saddened that my son did not feel comfortable enough to come out to me, yet I am not surprised. Part of me has always known he was gay; however, I am embarrassed to admit that deep down I wished it was not true. I have gay friends and family, and have never had a problem with whom people choose to love. But as a mother of a gay son, I was torn. First and foremost, I love my son with all my heart and soul and did not want him to ever be the subject of torment and hate. Secondly, I felt that perhaps it was somehow my fault because

I raised him by myself with little contact with his father. I worried far too much about how I would be judged, and Jim suffered because of it.

We cannot unscramble eggs, and I cannot undo my shortcomings as a parent. Anyone who has ever raised a child knows it is the most difficult, albeit rewarding, experience in life. I did not embrace Jim's true nature; instead, I made him go against his grain, pushing him in a direction he was so obviously not comfortable going. I signed him up for soccer, tennis, karate, and even wrestling. "There must be some sport he can excel in," I reasoned in my own mind. Despite the undeniable evidence to the contrary, I continued to focus on what I wanted him to be. No matter how hard I tried, he was more comfortable playing with toys associated with girls, a fact which mortified me.

I am not sure why, but I allowed him to participate in the local community theatre. I am grateful for that because I think it was the one outlet that gave him solace from my unyielding pressures to acquiesce to gender specific roles.

What upsets me most about the way I handled Jim's childhood is that he is truly a wonderful, funny, smart, loving, and gifted individual. Without realizing the consequences of my actions, I seemed to go out of my way to squelch those beautiful traits. Even worse, I unintentionally made him feel less than the amazing individual he is.

I cannot ever change the pain I caused my own son, and the guilt I feel will haunt me the rest of my life. But my hope for this book is that it will reach other parents of children who may be different, or anyone who knows someone who may be different, and maybe help them understand their loved ones better. By allowing our children, friends, or co-workers to be their authentic selves, the person God has made them to be, they have the freedom to blossom into the amazing individuals they are destined to be, and change this world in amazing ways.

2

Johanna's Story

I come from a conservative Christian background. My father was an ordained Baptist minister, and my mother was a licensed minister. I grew up theologically accepting strict evangelical teachings. As a teenager, I led Bible studies. After high school, I attended a Christian college. I was taught to believe that the Scriptures said homosexuality was a sin. Quite frankly, the issues related to homosexuality were not a top priority for me, since they did not impact my life.

When my son was in grade school, he and his friends played youth soccer. It was along the sidelines at games that I first met Larry Williams, the minister at a local church. I quickly developed respect for him and an appreciation of his knowledge of Scriptures, intelligence, humor, and engaging personality. Not long after that, my son and I started attending the church where Larry and his wife Jeri were co-pastors. My son was delighted, since he had become close friends with all three of their sons.

At their church, I met several individuals whom I came to love and admire, who just happened to be gay. Larry and I had many long discussions about homosexuality and whether or not it was a sin. He, too, was forced to look at Scriptures differently. I prayed often for answers. I learned the hard way that when you ask God for wisdom and insight, you sometimes have to be prepared to admit you have been wrong. That is just what happened to me.

Two people in our congregation come to mind, who continually demonstrated Christian love and service and obviously had the Holy Spirit upon them in a big way. And they happened to be homosexual. It was evident that God loved them and was using them. I also came to realize that the discrimination and hurt that they endured because of who they were had a pronounced impact on me; I felt responsible for speaking out against the prejudices.

My own grandparents died in Nazi concentration camps simply because of who they were; they were Jewish. I grew up keenly aware of anti-Semitic beliefs and learned we must speak out against them. The words of Martin Niemöller haunted me, "Then they came for me – and there was no one left to speak out for me." [1]

As I prayed for clarity about these amazing gay men, I came to realize that God does not make mistakes. God had brought these men into my life to change me. I could no longer dismiss their wounds and the prejudices against them because it did not impact me. By this time, my son was well into his teenage years. John Williams, my son's long-time friend, now openly acknowledged

---

[1] Niemöller, Martin, "First They Came – by Pastor Martin Niemöller," *Holocaust Memorial Day Trust*, publication date unknown, hmd.org.uk/resources/first-they-came-by-pastor-martin-niemoller/

that he was gay. This is the very same darling child who came to my home to play with my son, ate chocolate chip cookies, and watched movies with us. He certainly is a child of God as much as any of the other children. The point is, God does not make mistakes, and what God creates is good.

I also came to realize that in John 3:16-17, two verses that are cherished by believers, it says, "For God so loved the world that [God] gave [God's] only begotten Son, that whoever believes in [the Son] shall not perish, but have eternal life. For God did not send [God's] Son into the world to judge the world, but that the world might be saved through [the Son]." Those verses do not come with an asterisk excluding certain categories of people. The Scripture teaches that God's love is for ALL. Love is the key, not judgement.

Despite many ministers being defrocked for beliefs about openly loving and embracing those who are in the LGBTQ+ community, and despite the plethora of derogatory feedback she received from the anti-gay community, Jeri was always honest about what she felt the Holy Spirit told her about homosexuality. Her staunch beliefs about the subject helped me look at my own beliefs differently. She helped me be more compassionate towards everyone.

3

Steve's Story

My story is from the perspective of an ex-ex-gay, and how Drexel Hill Baptist Church helped me in my journey to help gay Kenyan Christians dispel the cloud of ignorance.

In October of 1997, at the age of 44, I abruptly left Faith Baptist Church of Sparta, New Jersey, for Jose, the person who is now my legal husband. (We were married in 2008 in California.) I had pastored faithfully for ten years, but was no longer willing to hide my true self, which was not permitted in the church.

Soon after leaving the ministry, as a theologian rooted in the evangelical faith, it became my priority and passion to study every scholarly book available on the topic of the Bible and homosexuality, both pro and con. I had no idea the church-at-large had been producing such studies for at least two decades.

Ten years later, in the summer of 2007, Jose and I did a live interview on the Bible and homosexuality with the Nairobi, Kenya, Kiss 100 Big Breakfast Show. Summarizing the broadcast, the July 18th *Nairobi Star* newspaper reported that Jose and I "believe the scriptures have been used to discriminate against homosexuals, alienating them from the church. They deny they are twisting the Bible to justify their claims."

One radio listener emailed me and said, "I was listening to you on the radio, and I must say, a job well done. You sent a real *[sic]* good message to many Kenyans. I applaud you for that. I was greatly inspired by what both of you had to say. For a long time I haven't considered myself a Christian because I felt so sinful ... until today. So, I greatly applaud you for opening my eyes, and many others out there that are like me."

Pastor Jeri Williams and her dear husband are the important practical link between my years of personal academic studies and that pivotal Kiss 100 radio interview in Nairobi, Kenya. In 2006, they pressed me to create a formal presentation of all the material on the Bible and homosexuality that I had been gathering in my head over the years. Because of them, I was given a platform on which to practice before a live audience. This was an incredible opportunity to clearly articulate my developing theology of the Bible and homosexuality.

In the fall of 2005, Jose and I came on board with Other Sheep as Coordinator for Africa and Asia, and Executive Director, respectively. Other Sheep, a multicultural, ecumenical, Christian ministry that works worldwide for the full inclusion of LGBTQ+ people of faith within their respective faith communities, did not yet have a presence in either Africa or Asia. Jose would pioneer Africa and Asia for Other Sheep.

Six months later in February of 2006, Jose and I met Pastor Jeri Williams, her husband, who is also an ordained minister and a scholar in his own right, and members of their Drexel Hill Baptist Church at an AWAB (Association of Welcoming and Affirming Baptists) weekend event hosted by Madison Avenue Baptist Church, in New York City. At the close of the event, they invited us to join them at a fast-food restaurant. It was over burgers and fries that Pastor Jeri invited me to give a one-day seminar at Drexel Hill Baptist Church on the Bible and homosexuality.

In an article I wrote shortly after this encounter for the online magazine, *Whosoever*, I reflected on Pastor Jeri's invitation,

> She asked me to bring to her church a four-hour Saturday seminar on the Bible and homosexuality. I believe she did so to cause me to stretch myself in ministry. What an assignment! I knew it would have to be a Power Point presentation, though I had never created a Power Point presentation before. And, never before had I heard myself speak out loud in front of an audience on what the Bible does or does not say about homosexuality. Nonetheless, she entered a date into her planning book: September 30th, seven months down the road.[2]

The summer following my Drexel Hill Baptist Church presentation, Jose and I embarked on our first trip to Nairobi, Kenya, at the invitation of Ishtar, an NGO HIV/AIDS education and prevention organization. The specific purpose of our journey was to

---

[2] Parelli, Stephen, "My Debt of Gratitude to a Welcoming Church and Queer Theologians," *Whosoever*, May 1, 2007, whosoever.org/v11i6/debt.html

work with Christian LGBTQ+ people who were on Ishtar's extensive roster of contacts. We rented an apartment within a walled complex with very tight security. There we conducted as many as three study groups a day with many gay Christians (and at least one Muslim) attending.

One of the countless things that we accomplished within these groups was the presentation of, and the distribution of, our Power Point studies on the Bible and homosexuality. This was the very same material we had presented at Drexel Hill Baptist Church, which had become our proving ground thanks to Pastor Jeri, her husband, and the members of her church.

With the experience of my initial presentation at Drexel Hill Baptist Church and our summer of educating the Kenyan LGBTQ+ Christians, I honed my research into a small definitive paper on the topic entitled "Taking Points - What You Need to Know and Say When They Say: 'But the Bible Clearly Condemns Homosexuality!'" It was published in 2012.

Those with whom we had worked and ministered in the summer of 2007 in Kenya had told us again and again, "Thank you, thank you! Your coming to Kenya has changed my life forever." The day we left to return to the States, a Christian gay couple gave us a card containing this heartfelt message, "We thank God for sending Jose and Steve to this country in such a time. We're blessed and going back to the glory that we'd left because of ignorance."

Drexel Hill Baptist Church and Reverend Dr. Jeri Williams helped me help gay Kenyan Christians overcome the ignorance.

4

Bob's Story

I grew up in a time and place where people, my family included, had derogatory names for every race and nationality. This was the jargon of my parents' generation and, I am sure, their parents' as well. It was intensified with all the immigrants coming into the country during the late 1940s and early 1950s, settling into neighborhoods of like ethnicity. I grew up in a very small country village. I was insulated from the real world. There was much that I did not know or understand firsthand. Any diversity was out of "the norm" and scorned, and those in the LBGTQ+ community, especially, were considered outcasts.

When I joined the Navy in the mid-1960s, I was thrown into a mix of ethnicities and sexual orientations. This was my first experience with homosexuals, though the terminology used back then to describe them was not so respectful. There were guys in boot camp who would hang around together very closely, a bit too closely for the rest of us. They were pretty much shunned and I am fairly certain they never made it through boot camp.

I was stationed in Pensacola, Florida, and spent my off time in Mobile, Alabama. In the men's room at the bus station, I was approached by a man who I suddenly realized was hitting on me. My opinion at that time in my life was that all homosexuals were predators who stalked young men. My first instinct was to fight. He chose to run.

Sometime later I was in San Diego, California, getting ready to board a ship for Viet Nam. I was again approached by a man in a bar. Some other sailors and I decided this was not the kind of establishment we wanted to patronize, so we left. This reinforced my opinion of all homosexuals. I was aware of this "behavior" going on after that, but was never approached again. However, my view of all homosexuals was set in stone after these experiences, and I would have nothing to do with them. This topic was something I would not speak of for many years.

In 1998, I moved to Drexel Hill, Pennsylvania, with my "significant other." We decided to try the church up the hill from our apartment. We felt very comfortable and welcomed from our first visit, with the exception of one of the musicians. He was obviously gay and made no attempt to hide it. As time went on and I got to know him better, I realized he did not fit the mold into which I had put all homosexuals. He would make jokes about being gay, and sometimes talk and act in a flamboyant manner, the way gay men are often stereotyped. But he never tried to push his sexual orientation on me. He is an extraordinary musician, but more than that and above all else, he is a faithful Christian.

I speak of this gentleman because he opened my eyes and heart to see people as PEOPLE first, not as the stereotypes with which

I was raised. There are others in our church from diverse backgrounds and cultures, with whom I have become friends over the years. There are many members of our church who are part of the LGBTQ+ community. There are mixed race families as well, who would never have been accepted in my small, 1950s, rural village. I have, over time, come to embrace these people as my friends and church family, not as people defined by the things that differentiate them from me.

Jeri would often preach on love and forgiveness. We are to love one another as Jesus teaches in the Bible. This is the consistent message of our church. No matter what our differences are, we are all the same in God's eyes.

In the hymn "Amazing Grace," one sentence fits my journey at church, "I once was lost but now am found, was blind, but now I see."

5

David's Story

My name is David and I am a chaplain at a level-one trauma center at an Ivy League university hospital in Philadelphia. I was born in the Richard Allen Projects and grew up in the Logan section of North Philadelphia. As a little boy, I sat through years of that unforgettable and haunting sermon, the one condemning me to an ungodly life of deviant behaviors, with the impossibility of ever truly receiving complete and total love from even God. So firmly established was this teaching in the church – even requiring compliance from my parents, who knew their child was different – that many were never able to surmount the trauma of the psycho-spiritual assault and separation the church had imposed, including me. Nor could we overcome the physical separation that was to follow. Like others, I knew without a doubt that it was I who had to change if I wanted to remain in the church and in relationship with God.

Today, I wonder if the church-at-large is troubled by the pain which that separation has generated. As my peers were made to believe, in fact warned about, our sexuality was our choice and would always be a choice. Even before sexual maturity set in, I was haunted by the thought, "was I to become that thing?" We were made to be vigilant of the oncoming wave of sexuality that would doom us if we became THAT.

Being that thing was not my choice. Consequently, I was thrust upon the same journey of self-hatred, spiritual confusion, anger, and resentment that almost all gay youth experience. Growing up in the Baptist Church, I did not observe joyful, open, well-adjusted, not-in-hiding, reconciled, godly, gay men as congregational leaders, worshiping and embracing who they were in Jesus Christ. Moreover, I rarely see it today. In myself, I discern it. And God has called me to be this to others.

I met Jeri in 2003. I had purchased a house near Drexel Hill, Pennsylvania, after finishing my bachelor's degree in vocal performance at Boston University. I began travelling up and down State Road, in Drexel Hill, to get to the highway or the market. One day while I was driving this road, I saw a karaoke sign in front of some building. It read, "Karaoke Every Friday Night." I thought, "Who hosts karaoke on Friday nights?" For years I did not see anything but the karaoke sign. I never saw that it was a church. I passed by that karaoke sign regularly and each time, something kept nudging me to look at it more closely. "Look up. Look up." In retrospect, it was exasperating to be actively ignoring that sign for so long, and also the church to which it was connected. One day driving by the karaoke sign once again, I finally looked up. It was a CHURCH ... a BAPTIST Church. It was Drexel Hill Baptist Church. Immediately I said to God, "You know I can't go in there, right? I'm still gay." I looked right at God as if God did not remember. But God did remember and, as clearly as I am writing this story, God said "I want you to do this. You are to attach your name upon it." And so I have.

One day I walked in and sat down. I sat silently in the back for two years, hardly saying anything to anyone. I saw the interracial couples and those that were clearly gay and lesbian. But I was Black and gay, and the price would be much higher for me if I erred. I waited for THAT sermon. Each week, I was ready to storm out in an indignant and pious huff at THAT sermon – or if someone said something I found to be homo-hateful (not homophobic – call it what it is). But THAT sermon never came. Now I had to stay.

Not only did I stay, but I became involved in both the spiritual and the social life of the church, which helped me discover my calling to ministry. In the John Stevenson Hall School of Ministry, under Rev. Dr. Jeri E Williams and Rev. Lawrence A. Williams, I endeavored, like many other seminarians, to explore and delve into an increased understanding of the nature of God. Consequently, eight years, ninety-six credit hours, and over thirty-three classes later, I commanded a breadth of knowledge, and approached Andover Newton Theological School, which was founded by Baptists in 1825.

I was raised in a godly home with a strong faith and a personal relationship with God. I considered myself a faithful Christian, even though the church shunned me for years. Now I was at a crossroads. Would this institution, steeped in Baptist traditions, welcome me, a gay, Black man? Just as with Drexel Hill Baptist Church, I waited for THAT letter, the one that said I was not the right "type" for their school. That letter never came. Instead, a letter of acceptance arrived, and I knew I was on my way to fulfilling God's calling in my life.

I have stood with Jeri each Sunday since 2006. Our journey with God has been amazing. I will have finished my Master of Divinity degree at Andover Newton Theological School by the time this book goes to print. I am also newly inducted into the Jonathan Edwards Society, the school's honor society. I am honored to be God's servant in a time such as this, where God's queer children, the weirdos, the throwaways, and the disinvited are ushered back into the pews where they rightfully belong, and back into communion with God.

It is clear to those of us who have always been different, whether gay, lesbian, bisexual, asexual, intersex, unisex, no sex, or any other variety of God's other sheep, that any discussion of homosexual nature vs. nurture is simply irrelevant. We are whom we are, and God made us that way. GOD is OUR GOD too. My life, itself, confirms this. Being quietly and superficially tolerated is not love. I see us, silent and invisible, living a covertly religious existence, even among contemporaries. It is time for us, the other sheep, to live authentically as the individuals God created us to be. We must be free to follow our call, whatever that may be, even if that means a call to ministry.

Through the spiritual support of Jeri and The Green Church, as well as my own prayer and reflection, I acknowledge that my calling is to be a healer of the "whosoevers," not much different than Jesus, who sought out the outcasts. I will be a healer through song and through character, through empathy and forgiveness, knowing I am one of their own.

6

Dan's Story

While my husband John and I were at the Pride Festival, in Philadelphia, we found ourselves at the Drexel Hill Baptist Church / Fusion table. We met a few of the members from the church who were staffing the table. We are from Drexel Hill, Pennsylvania, and never knew that there was a welcoming and affirming church in our area. We decided to attend the next service and meet the pastors.

We were immediately made to feel like we were at home and welcomed. Pastor Jeri and Pastor Larry would become two of the most influential people in our faith journeys. We met with Pastor Jeri and she gave us our spiritual gifts test as well as a personality profile questionnaire to see how our talents might be best used to help the church. Pastor Jeri had us each take some of the courses offered by the church, which she and her husband Larry taught. It was in these classes that I learned how and when to use my voice.

They also gave me the knowledge I needed in order to back up my opinions and present informed arguments. During this time, I joined the new John Stephenson Hall School of Ministry, which the church had established. This gave me a chance to learn, while reigniting my passion for ministry. I took as many classes as I could from both Pastor Jeri and Pastor Larry.

While taking these classes, I had the opportunity to preach at a Good Friday service. As one might expect, my nerves were getting the better of me as I sat waiting to deliver my very first sermon. We had all been encouraged to pause and offer a prayer before beginning, which most clergy do. While most of my classmates started off with, "Let's pray," I was not as eloquent. I simply said, "Pray," in a very commanding tone, which brought a chuckle from many attending the service. I do not think I will ever live that down.

During this time, a friend of mine from high school died of AIDS. He was not given the lifesaving information on protecting himself. This set off an anger in me, which sparked a passion to never let that happen again. In 2006, with the help of Pastor Jeri, other people from our church, and the Unitarian Universalist Church of Delaware County, we created an LGBTQ+ youth center in Delaware County. This center provided an online resource center which the youth of the county could access for a variety of information, including the information that just might have saved my friend.

When the church moved from Drexel Hill to the rural area where it is now, we were not able to get to the new church because of family and transportation issues. While away from the church, we never joined another faith community. Occasionally, we attended a service at another church that was pastored by one of our friends, or as a guest of someone who invited us to their church. None of them ever seemed to fit. When John and I were looking to make our marriage legal in the state of Pennsylvania, we reached out to a few of our pastor friends and contacts. The only three who would do the marriage service included our old pastor from Philadelphia, Pastor Jeri, and Rev. Eddie, an associate pastor at The Green Church. When we asked Pastor Jeri to do our wedding, we knew we had to return to that church. We knew it was our church home.

In those two years when we were unable to attend The Green Church, I studied everything on farming and sustainability that I could find. I thought it was because of the new *Practical Preppers* television show, on which I had gotten quite literally "hooked." Evidently however, it was God preparing me to help when we got back to the church. The Green Church started a farm, and my passion and knowledge of farming and sustainability is now being used for the good of the community. Now we are home, and that is where we plan to stay.

—7—

John's Story

I was kicked out of my church for being gay. I had been involved with the youth and taught Sunday school. I was confronted by the pastor and a few other men of the church. They asked me to leave the church because they thought I was a bad influence on the youth. I was heartbroken and felt really let down. These were people I looked up to and respected, and they turned me away with no regard for my spiritual or emotional health or wellbeing. That hurt … deeply.

I was so crushed by that experience that I did not go to church for about seven years. How could I ever face that rejection again? Then I met my future husband who told me about the church he was attending. I decided to give it a try. I went to that church for two years and then left because of a disagreement.

By chance, or more accurately, by God's grace, we found Drexel Hill Baptist Church. Dan and I discovered the church at a Pride event. I did not know there was an accepting church in Drexel Hill. I had lived in Drexel Hill all my life and did not know that the church right around the corner would accept me with open arms just as I was.

This was a church where I was welcomed and loved. This is the place I called home. The first time I attended worship there, I felt at peace and at home. I attended the church for eight years and was heavily involved. I took several classes and even taught Sunday school. I was not excluded from leadership because of my sexual orientation. It was great. I finally found my church family. But then the church moved, and we were not able to go because of the distance.

Two years later, my husband and I returned to the church that I called home. I was finally home again, welcomed as family. I am back home and finally feel like I am part of a family that accepts me. The church is full of such wonderful people, and I am proud and honored to call them my friends and FAMILY. I am so looking forward to seeing the great things that I can do to help the church's mission.

I would not be where I am today, in terms of my relationship with God and involvement in the church, if it were not for Jeri Williams. I love her so much. She is one of the most loving, caring, and accepting people I know. She has so much love to offer everyone. She touches so many people's lives, mine included. I admire and look up to her. She taught me to accept myself and to not let people get to me. Being around her, I feel this warmth, and I know I am safe. There is just something about her that dispels the "stuff" that is holding me down. She always says, "Honey, you're a wonderful person and you have a lot to offer." When I fall, she is there. She helps me up and then hugs me with one of her famous embraces that brings me encouragement and support.

It is such a great feeling to be loved so unconditionally. I can always come and talk to her, and she always listens. She is real, genuine, and she brings out the best in me. I love to draw, so now she has me drawing caricatures for different church members. She wants to have them all displayed on the wall, which I think will bring joy to everyone who comes into the church. That makes me exceedingly happy. She is a wonderful person, pastor, leader, mother, and friend. I am honored to call her my friend. I am so glad that I finally came home and am here to stay. I am excited and eagerly looking forward to following her on this journey.

8

Terri's Story

There I sat. It was 1967; I was with my brother at the Cathedral of Saints Peter and Paul, our parish church. Although I was only six years old, the priest caught my attention as he talked about Jesus' death and resurrection. I felt an immediate awareness of the importance of Christ's sacrifice. I remember thinking, "Why do I have to wait to take communion?" I did not need to process up the aisle with everyone else. I defied my brother and all the others around me and went to the communion rail. Surprisingly and without question, the priest offered me the wafer, and I took it. I attended Catholic school and went to church, but never accepted all the ritual and intermediary saints for which the church was known. I believed in talking directly to God.

In January of 1975, when I was fourteen years old, my mother died. That night I told Jesus that someday, somehow, I would serve God. The following March I was introduced to a new church, called The

Way. They were evangelizing on the University of Pennsylvania campus. I joined them, going to northern Pennsylvania on summer mission trips and eventually moving with them to New York to help open a new headquarters. My passion for Jesus was exploding and, even though I was ridiculed by friends and family, I had to follow the path on which God was leading me. This church was the only place I felt accepted and loved, since my friends and family had basically turned their backs on me because of my desire to serve God.

I was married at the age of twenty. By the time I was twenty-three, I had two little girls and was separated from my husband. It was at this point that I began questioning my sexuality. I was starting to put pieces of a puzzle together in my life. Through grade school I had crushes on some of the nuns, not to mention one particular girl in my school. It was all beginning to make sense, in an uncomfortable sort of way.

Not knowing quite where to turn, I went back to the Catholic Church, though I was not happy there. I subsequently left and did not attend church for a long time.

Over the years, I tried to return to the Catholic Church, but every time I felt I was living in the shadows. I had accepted my sexuality, but I was not open about it. In May of 2002, my wife and I moved in together to care for our son. We had been together for about three years, but had known each other for about seventeen years. We were beginning a new journey together and had a little boy to think about. He had many issues and was a sickly child. I did not want him raised Catholic, but wanted him to know Jesus. My wife was Christian, too, which was very important to me.

She first started attending Drexel Hill Baptist Church, and even took our son, on occasion. She saw an article about Pastor Jeri and the church being "gay friendly." I was certain of two things: I wanted our son to know Jesus, and I wanted him to be raised knowing that it was okay to be gay. I eventually started to go to church with them.

At that time, a new class was starting at the church specifically designed for the LGBTQ+ community. I started to realize that Jeri was completely convinced that Jesus loved everyone just as they are. Although I knew that Jesus loved me, I still was not convinced I would be in heaven. I was having a difficult time coming to terms with my faith and my sexuality.

Larry, Jeri's husband and co-pastor of the church, taught a class with about twelve or thirteen of us. After a few weeks of introductions and becoming acquainted with one another, questions began to surface. Someone asked Larry, "Do you think being gay is a sin?" When he answered, "Yes," he never anticipated the effect it would have on me and the others in the class. My stomach dropped. Anger filled me, followed by hurt. I had to leave the room and pull myself together. Sin is anything that hurts or goes against Jesus; it is something you should be able to change. But all of us knew we could not change our sexuality; this is how God made us.

After a short time and a chance for us to gain our composure, we all gathered together to discuss the topic further. Larry did not realize how his comment impacted all of us. But, each of us had some kind of story or reaction, which would drive Larry to look into what Scripture really had to say about homosexuality. We all found it curious that, if this topic was so important, and homosexuality was such a grave sin, why did Jesus never say anything about it?

I came to respect Larry as a man of God and grew to love him as a person and a friend. After years of studying Scripture, Larry began to understand that being gay was not a sin. As the years went by, my wife and I grew close to Pastors Larry and Jeri. We attended Christian events, as well as social events, together.

My wife and I wanted to be legally married. So after talking with us, both Larry and Jeri agreed to officiate, reminding us that marriage is not to be entered into lightly, and they would hold us accountable. Gay marriage was not legal in Pennsylvania at that time, so I would not be able to have the church wedding for which I had always hoped. We were married by Pastors Larry and Jeri in Punta Cana. In May of 2014, three days after gay marriage became legal in Pennsylvania, Pastor Jeri married my wife and me at The Green Church.

I know that I am a child of God. I am loved by God. I look forward to seeing all my brothers and sisters in heaven. Through The Green Church and Jeri's love and friendship over these many years, I have come to know fully that God is not judging me because of my sexuality.

9

Jonathan's Story

I met Jeri and Larry when I started attending the Fusion Church service in Center City Philadelphia. I had been church hopping for a while and could not find the right fit. There are plenty of churches that are welcoming and affirming of gay people in the city, but I somehow felt like I did not belong.

I think a church should feel as natural as being around your family. I have been to churches that feel like an awkward grade school dance when the service ends, and you try your best to make conversation with those around you but you really cannot wait to leave. At Fusion/Drexel Hill Baptist/The Green Church, it immediately felt like a family. It felt real and natural and beautiful. We were a diverse bunch of authentic people who wanted to worship together and try to figure out what we were supposed to do in this life.

Jeri does not just approve of gay people, she fully accepts, affirms, and embraces them. Have you ever had a hug from Jeri? She pulls you in and asks how you are doing, and tells you that she's been thinking about you. She is such a true reflection of God's love – for everyone.

10

Latifah's Story

I stumbled upon Fusion Baptist Church in late summer 2008 by typing "open and affirming churches in Pennsylvania" into the search engine, and *VOILA!* I was jaded with the rules of a "normal" church and needed a church where love and faith are the centerpiece. I set a date to check the church out, and when I arrived, I was very surprised. I was astonished because everyone was dressed down and the pastor was a woman. I thought, "Wow, way to rebel against tradition! This is my kind of place." In my previous experience with the traditional African American churches, neither of these things would have been acceptable. I felt like this was a place where I could be quite comfortable. Eventually, I migrated from the evening service at Fusion Baptist to the main Sunday morning service at Drexel Hill Baptist. The rest, as they say, is history.

Over the years, I got to know the Williams family very well. Since becoming a member in 2008, the church has become family to me. They were there for me when I lost everything in a fire in 2013. My church family made me feel as if I never lost anything. They truly helped me to get through a terrible situation. Jeri and Larry allowed me and my spouse to live in the church parsonage until we were able to get on our feet. To me, that was, and still is, the true form of what it means to be a Christ follower. Our church exemplifies true hospitality in its most basic and uncomplicated form. Jeri, as the shepherd of the church, embodies the truest essence of being a Christian. I am grateful to be in the company of such a great woman.

Contributors

Rev. Dr. Jeri Williams

Rev. Dr. Jeri E. Williams, Author

Rev. Dr. Jeri Williams started the first gay Baptist Church in the United States, called "Fusion," in 2001. Since then, she has counseled hundreds of people in the LGBTQ+ community who have struggled with the idea that God did not love them because of their sexual orientation. Many wanted to serve God and go into the ministry themselves, only to discover they would never be accepted into seminary.

Rev. Dr. Jeri Williams has been an American Baptist Pastor for over thirty years. She has been an ally and advocate for the LGBTQ+ community for more than twenty of those years. A lifelong champion for the marginalized, she began working with convicts and addicts while she was still in college, working toward her undergraduate degree in psychology. She also joined in the civil rights movement. When she felt the call to ministry in an era when women were not accepted as leaders in the church, she fought for women's equality in ministry through biblical study and research. Now she has, again, been called by the Holy Spirit to fight for the rights of those considered "less than" – the LGBTQ+ community.

At a time when most of Christendom preached that homosexuality was a sin, one of her sons came out to her and her husband (also an American Baptist pastor). Thankfully, Dr. Williams' son knew from her preaching and teaching that God loves all of God's children, and we should accept how God has made each of us. This accepting and loving attitude made her son feel comfortable enough to reveal his authentic self at an early age.

It is amazing how God prepared her for the day her son came out. It is an understatement to say that her views were not popular. And they still are not. She has received death threats over her views from those who profess to love God. It is an enigma to her that there are still people today who say they love God while hating those who profess differing or opposing beliefs.

She believes God has called her to help others (the LGBTQ+ community, families of the LGBTQ+, clergy, lay people, congregations, or anyone who is struggling with whether homosexuality is a sin or not) to re-evaluate their view and interpretation of scripture.

Rose DeLone

Rose DeLone, Coauthor

Rose DeLone is a full-time sales specialist, blogger, and freelance writer. She has written several articles for *The Wood River Press*, *The Charlestown Press*, and *The Westerly Sun* in Rhode Island. She attended Reading Area Community College, majoring in communications. Rose is a prolific writer and perpetual student of words.

Rose and Rev. Williams met in high school and have been close friends all these years. When Jeri told her about this project, she was delighted to take on the role of co-author to help bring this labor of love to fruition. She currently lives in eastern Pennsylvania.

Rev. Patricia Pitzer

Rev. Patricia Pitzer, Editor

Rev. Patricia Pitzer is a graduate of Palmer Theological Seminary with a Master of Divinity degree. She and her husband joined Drexel Hill Baptist Church in 1991, when they were married by Rev. Dr. Jeri Williams and her husband Rev. Lawrence A. Williams. She was ordained in 2009 by Larry and Jeri.

Pat was an adjunct professor at Palmer Theological Seminary, teaching Writing for Seminarians and Biblical Greek, until she moved to the west coast. She has served as an Associate Pastor and Director of Women's Ministries at Drexel Hill Baptist Church, as well as Administrative Director and Acting Executive Director for Francis House Center, a Sacramento, California, nonprofit that served the homeless. It was here at Francis House that she was lovingly given the title, "The Grammar Police."

Now retired, Pat resides in eastern Pennsylvania with her husband, near her children and grandchildren.